Hiding in Time
Too Many Secrets

By

Charles Royals

Hiding in Time

By the time you reach the end of this book the information you are about to receive will keep you from closing your eyes at night. People hold all kind of secrets, some things are kept quiet and personal that may be innocent in nature and just embarrassing in some circumstances. The same way some secrets only hurt pride or reputation other secrets are life altering or even deadly to society. Many times people take extreme measures to keep or hide secrets. It has been said by many the only way two people can keep a secret is if one of them are dead. This does not appear to be true anymore; people find innovative way and means of keeping secrets. Most people believe only the rich or affluent, people with criminal intent; politicians and government officials keep deadly secrets. But also sometimes it may be your doctor, police officer, school teacher, scout master, or religious leaders that are keeping life altering and deadly secrets. Keeping secrets people are subjected to fear, extortion, payoffs, physical and mental abuse, sexual abuse or even death.

Charles A. Royals

Table of Contents

Chapter One

No Questions Asked

The American people place their trust in their institutions public and private. The American people believe in a society of equality, justice and fairness based on faith, morals and values. People place trust in those who display integrity, honesty and leadership openly in the eyes of society in public while respecting individual privacy. However once someone becomes a public figure their life becomes an open book, and that is when secrets become the most important part of many lives. The secrets some people keep hidden many times will make the difference in prosperity and achievement or failure and desolation. People will hide their secrets beneath days, weeks and many times years of false perception only allowing society to see one side of their true being. Long time secrets has brought the country to the brinks of disaster after the people learned of Presidential corruption during the seventy's and the eighty's and ninety's.

Several men of the highest integrity, with strong morals and values in the eyes of the public were elected to the highest political office in the land. Not only did these men have secrets of great embarrassment but criminal in nature. History has proved to us that we never really know anyone not even our closest friend or next door neighbour. There are secrets inside families; some are known by all family members, but some only known by a few or the one. The worst the secret the closer it's kept.

No one knows what anyone may have been capable of at any point in their life, or what they may be hiding, or how long they have been keeping it hidden from society. Hidden secrets caused disruption within our country's government at critical times. Many of us can remember events in time no one wanted to believe, however the facts made it perfectly clear the country was being deceived. Some of us can remember the 1960's two men the country believed to be of great integrity help office in the White House. President John F. Kennedy and Vice President Lyndon B, Johnson. President Kennedy was love and respected by the entire country. However no one in the country knew President Kennedy was the keeper of three secrets that would have a devastating effect on the security of the country.

There were rumors of the president having an extra marital affair with movie star Marilyn Monroe, allegations that were never officially investigated or proven. The second of President Kennedy's secrets was he suffered from a chronic medical condition that put him through extreme pain to the extent he sometimes could not function or perform his duties. However the Presidential medical staff and his cabinet administration were up to the challenge of covering for him at all cost. The third of President Kennedy's secrets was a deal he made with the Russian President to stop nuclear weapons from being based in Cuba. However that was one secret that prevented nuclear conflict and possible World War.

However with all his faults and virtues of his secrets President Kennedy was assonated in 1963. Lyndon Johnson became President after Kennedy's death. Mourning the death of a man well love by all, the country placed their faith and trust in a man they thought would do no wrong. But little did anyone know Lyndon Johnson had secrets of his own. Many of the American people remember the Viet Nam War and President Lyndon Johnson's involvement, but not all of the facts. In 1964 presidential election, Johnson was chided by the Republican candidate, Barry Goldwater, for being too soft in his approach to the North Vietnamese." "In response, Johnson told the public that he was not prepared to send US troops thousands of miles overseas to do what the South Vietnamese Army should be doing and protecting its people." Johnson convinced the American public he was against the Viet Nam conflict.

Johnson's statements were the primary reason he "won the 1964 presidential election with ease." "It was not long before US troops were sent to South Vietnam." "In early 1965, Johnson authorized 'Operation Rolling Thunder', which started on February 24th." "This was the wholesale bombing of North Vietnam and NLF-held territory in South Vietnam."." "March 8th 1965, 3,500 US Marines and combat troops arrived in South Vietnam." "Johnson sold this deployment to the public by claiming they would be in South Vietnam as a short-term measure."

The escalation of aggression ended a conflict and was the beginning of the Viet Nam War. According to Johnson message to America "Initially Operation Rolling Thunder was meant to last for eight weeks," however the escalation "lasted three years." ["Johnson could never have envisaged what he had started." "By the time of the 1968 presidential election, America had become embroiled in a war that was to take on far greater dimensions than anyone could have believed in 1965."] According to Trueman, C. N. "Johnson did not stand for the 1968 presidential election and many pundits at the time stated that this was the result of what was happening to US troops in South Vietnam at the time." However there are things about the war in Viet Nam many people do not know?

The Viet Nam War was based on a lie perpetrated "by the president of the United States" Lyndon Johnson. Another secret kept from the American public is a company owned by Lyndon Johnson was paid millions of dollars to drudge the bay in Viet Nam for the United States Navy War ships without voting on the contract. This brings back the original question the public needs answers, Why Lie? Lyndon Johnson wasn't the first or the only president to lie to the American public nor will he be the last. Two men of honor left the country looking for leadership they could have trust. Three Presidents in a row left the country in need of a leader with strong ethics, impeccable integrity, morale and values they could believe in. However what the country wanted and what they would get shook the country to its core. Lyndon Johnson would not run for a second term and the people elected the biggest scandal in American history. Richard Nixon became President of the United States and Watergate was his secret. Richard Nixon's secret was exposed by two reporters from the Washington Post Newspaper Woodward and Bernstein leaving the country with a picture of Nixon people will never forget.

. Richard Nixon left the office of the president in disgrace, resigning to avoid impeachment. Richard Nixon's last address to the public he stated "I am not a crook" even though he accepted a pardon from President Ford that contradicted that statement with the fact only the guilty need a pardon. All efforts were in place to impeach Nixon at the time he resigned Nixon was well known for his v for victory sign but this time he could not win. "The articles of impeachment were passed only by the Committee on the Judiciary. They were never voted on in the full House of Representatives." "Nixon was not impeached. Analysis of the Judiciary Committee Votes by Political Party" and "Article 1" of Impeachment ["Resolved, That Richard M. Nixon, President of the United States, is impeached for high crimes and misdemeanors."

"Following articles of impeachment to be exhibited to the Senate: Articles of Impeachment Exhibited by the House of Representatives of the United States of America in the name of itself of all the people of the United States of America, against Richard M. Nixon, President of the United States of America, in Maintenance and Support of its Impeachment against him for High Crimes and Misdemeanors."] ["In his conduct of the office of President of the United States, Richard M. Nixon, in violation of his constitutional oath faithfully to execute the office of President of the United States and, to the best of his ability, preserve, protect, and defend the Constitution of the United States.

And also in violation of his constitutional duty to take care that the laws be faithfully executed, has prevented, obstructed, and impeded the administration of justice, in that: On June 17, 1972, and prior thereto, agents of the Committee for the Re-election of the President committed unlawful entry of the headquarters of the Democratic National Committee in Washington, District of Columbia, for the purpose of securing political intelligence."] However, once again Money, Politics, and Time allowed the affluent to walk away in shame but free of being held accountable for their actions. During the months before Nixon left office another secret was exposed. It was reviled that Richard Nixon was a chronic alcoholic that would talk to dead presidents throughout the White House. After Richard Nixon and Watergate the country wanted more transparency when it came to trusting electing officials.

The people begun to look beyond politicians to find people they believed would be trustworthy. The people begun to look up to people they believed to be well known and honest. A movie star whose name had become a household word became Governor of California, and the people believed his life was an open book and everyone knew and trusted him. Ronald Reagan, became US president in 1981, little did anyone know Reagan was hiding health secrets. Health issues are personal and kept confidential between a doctor and their patient, and no one had reason to question President Reagan's health. But it was many other things Reagan got involved that he kept secret.

President Reagan was implacably opposed to the Sandinista government after social unrest spread to neighboring countries." "In El Salvador, guerrilla fighters from the Farabundo Marti Liberation Front became involved in a conflict with the Salvadoran army, and a long and civil war between the army and left-wing rebels erupted in Guatemala."] According to reports, "Reagan quite openly allocated funds to the contras and to the CIA for the purpose of" destabilizing the "Sandinista regime." However, "opposition to this funding grew among the US public. In 1986, the Reagan government, secretly and illegally, transferred to the contras the proceeds of clandestine sales of military equipment supplied to Iran." Media "journalists exposed" the story and "congressional opposition to the funding of the contras grew, and eventually Washington was forced to stop." ["Reagan's policies failed, the Sandinistas were not overthrown militarily and the left-wing guerrillas were not defeated in either El Salvador or Guatemala, though here they were seriously weakened."

"Unpopular by the need to fight a long and costly war against the US backed contras, Sandinistas were unexpectedly voted out of office in elections in February 1990," and in El Salvador and Guatemala the guerrillas failed to achieve a military victory." "Both forces negotiated peace agreements putting down their arms."] After a decade of wars, it appears "unbelievable these tiny countries could have been seen by Reagan as a major threat to US national security."

Although no matter how it may appear "indirectly and fortuitously, Reagan achieved his underlying aim, which was to stop socialism spreading to the rest of Central America." However Reagan's actions needed Congressional approval which he never received. Many people see Reagan as a hero as if he never committed a crime, but a crime is a crime and a lie is a lie as with the first President George Bush. It is one thing to believe in lower taxes and use it for a campaign platform, but entirely different when a direct promise is made to the public. More than a year Bush campaigned on lower taxes for the American people something he knew would influence voters. However as fate would have it Bush guaranteed the public there would be no taxes. Bush openly lied to the public about tax increases by making the statement "Read my lips, no new taxes" that ultimately was the factor in his winning the election.

After taking office one of the first things Bush did was to raise taxes across the board on all Americans, and then entered a war in the Middle East. Bill Clinton came into office turning a deficit into a surplus rebuilding America's economy, but his moral convictions were questionable and created a sex scandal in the White House. Bill Clinton's secret sex life created a big gap separating the country politically. However sex secrets were not the only thing that was alleged that Clinton was keeping a secret. During the Whitewater and other investigations Clinton was exposed having an affair with an intern that led to him committing perjury.

Clinton made a false statement under oath when he said "I did not have sex with that woman." Clinton's lie led to his impeachment "by the House of Representatives," although Clinton was saved "by the senate and" finished out his term as president.

He was once the
WORST.
PRESIDENT.
EVER.
UNTIL TRUMP

George Bush number two the 42nd President was convinced to tell the public there were weapons of mass destruction in Iraq entering the country to a second war. Putting the country in recession with a busted deficit this too was proven to be untrue. However Bush was elected to a second term in office by some questionable voting in Florida conducted by his brother Jeb Bush.

Chapter Two

Everyone has a Secret

Secrets are not exclusively for the rich and powerful more than politicians keep secrets some even darker than anyone can imagine. People in every profession keep secrets, even those we think we know or closest to us. Over the years it has been reviled many high profile people in society has kept deep dark secrets, some even deadly. People highly visible in our neighborhoods, communities and cities we believe we know or have known for years we really don't know at all, or what secrets they are keeping.

Many people in America still remember John Wayne Gacy an outgoing citizen in his Chicago community, where he was known for his sociability and his performance as a clown at charitable events and children's' parties. But also Gacy had deep dark secrets that priced the hearts of the American people. According to Jenkins, J. P. "Gacy was born into a blue-collar family and seems to have had a fairly ordinary childhood." But that was no secret, what was unknown to most people Gacy ["exhibited a growing tendency toward sadism, which resulted in several encounters with the law in the 1960s. In 1968, after his conviction for sexually assaulting a teenage boy, he was confined in the Iowa State Men's Reformatory (Anamosa State Penitentiary) and forced to undergo psychological evaluation. After his release in 1970 and while still on parole, he was again arrested for sexual assault, but the charges were later dropped.

Gacy then became a fairly successful independent contractor and bought a house in suburban Chicago."] Over the years Gacy appeared to be an ordinary hard working citizen active in his church and community. Gacy acted as a scout master trusted with children and always willing to help others. However there were a number of young men that vanished in thin air from different parts of the country never to be found. No on earth expected Gacy until ["1978, after one of Gacy's victims was reported missing, police learned Gacy was the last person known to have seen him.

After obtaining a search warrant, police discovered the bodies of 29 boys and young men in a crawl space beneath Gacy's house."] Gacy's hidden secret was now public and his true nature exposed. That area of the house had emitted a foul stench for years, and only Gacy knew why? But Gacy ["told his houseguests and his wife that the smell was the result of moisture buildup. At his trial Gacy's plea of innocent by reason of insanity was supported by the testimony of several psychologists, who diagnosed him as schizophrenic, but was rejected by the jury, which found him guilty of all 33 murders of which he was accused; he was executed by lethal injection."] Most people are judged and accepted by first impression that unfortunately many times prove to be wrong. Nothing could make this truer than "In February 1980, Ted Bundy married Carole Ann Boone, a mother-of-two whom he'd dated before his secret was exposed and his initial arrest."

Carole Ann Boon joined hands with Bundy in a Florida courtroom during the penalty phase of his trial. "When Boone gave birth to a daughter in 1982, she named Ted Bundy as the father. Boone eventually realized Bundy was guilty of the crimes and stopped visiting him during the last two years of his imprisonment." Ted Bundy's secret was not one of his own; it started years before with his mother. ["Ted Bundy was born in Burlington, Vermont on November 24, 1946, starting life as his mother's secret shame." Eleanor Cowell was 22 years old and unmarried when she had her son Theodore, which humiliated her deeply religious parents.

She delivered the child at a home for unwed mothers in Vermont and later brought her son to her parents in Philadelphia. Hiding the fact Ted was an illegitimate child; he was raised as an adopted child of his grandparents and told his mother was his sister. Ted's mother moved with him to Tacoma, Washington, a couple years later. In 1951, she married Johnnie Bundy and the couple had several children together. From all appearances, Bundy grew up in a content, working-class family."] Ted Bundy showed an unhealthy interest in the macabre at an early childhood age. When Bundy was a little over three – years -old, he asserted a fascinated for knives and other sharp objects. Bundy was very shy but bright and did well in school, but not with other children. When Bundy grew into his teenage years, "a darker side of his character started to emerge." Bundy became a peeping tom and found pleasure and enjoyment peering through "other people's windows and thought nothing of stealing things he wanted from other people."

After Bundy became a "student at the University of Washington he fell in love with a wealthy young woman from California." This young lady provided everything he wanted: money, class, status and influence. Bundy was devastated after their breakup and blamed her for his fall from grace. Bundy selected most of his victims because they resembled his college girlfriend; attractive young students with long, dark hair and well-built bodies. Bundy's killings usually followed the same gruesome pattern of rage and hate.

"He often raped his victims before beating them to death." According to Biography, Bundy ["graduated from University of Washington with a degree in psychology in 1972 and had been accepted to law school in Utah. By the mid-1970s, Bundy had transformed himself, becoming more outwardly confident and active in social and political matters. Bundy even got a letter of recommendation from the Republican governor of Washington after working on his campaign. Ted Bundy admitted to 36 killings of young women across several states in the 1970s, but experts believe that the final tally may be closer to 100 or more."] The exact number of women Bundy killed will never been known, Ted Bundy took his deepest secrets to his grave. However Ted Bundy was not the only one to die with secrets. Some secrets were not buried but eaten. "Jeffrey Dahmer born May 21, 1960 died November 28, 1994) a serial killer that took the lives of 17 males between 1978 and 1991."

Jeffrey Dahmer was born in Milwaukee to Lionel and Joyce Dahmer. Jeffrey was ["an energetic and happy child until the age of 4, when surgery to correct a double hernia seemed to effect a change in the boy. Noticeably subdued, he became increasingly withdrawn following the birth of his younger brother and the family's frequent moves. By his early teens, he was disengaged, tense and largely friendless."] ["Dahmer claims that his compulsions toward necrophilia and murder began around the age of 14, but it appears that the breakdown of his parents' marriage and their acrimonious divorce.

Jeffery's change came a few years later may have been the catalyst for turning these thoughts into actions."] Dahmer's first murder occurred just after graduating high school, in June 1978, when he picked up a hitchhiker named Steven Hicks and took him home to his parents' house. Dahmer proceeded to get the young man drunk; when Hicks tried to leave, Dahmer killed him by striking him in the head and strangling him with a barbell. He dismembered the corpse of his first victim, packed the body parts in plastic bags and buried them behind his parents' home. Dahmer's alcohol consumption had spun out of control. He dropped out of school at Ohio State University after one quarter term, and his recently remarried father insisted that he join the Army. Dahmer's drinking problem persisted, and in early 1981, the Army discharged him.

Although German authorities would later investigate possible connections between Dahmer and murders that took place in the area during that time, it is not believed that he took any more victims while serving in the Armed Forces. Following his discharge, Dahmer returned home to Ohio. An arrest later that year for disorderly conduct prompted his father to send Dahmer to live with his grandmother in Wisconsin, but his alcohol problem continued and he was arrested the following summer for indecent exposure. He was arrested again in 1986, when two boys accused him of masturbating in front of them, and he received a one-year probationary sentence. September 1987 that Dahmer took his second victim, Steven Tuomi.

They checked into a hotel room and drank, and Dahmer eventually awoke to find Tuomi dead, with no memory of the previous night's activities. He bought a large suitcase to transport Tuomi's body to his grandmother's basement, where he dismembered and masturbated on the corpse before disposing of the remains. Dahmer killed two more victims at his grandmother's home. Dahmer's grandmother grew tired of his late nights and drunkenness, although she had no knowledge of his other activities she forced him to move out. September 1989, Dahmer had an extremely lucky escape: An encounter with a 13-year-old Laotian boy resulted in charges of sexual exploitation and second-degree sexual assault for Dahmer. He pleaded guilty, claiming that the boy had appeared much older. While awaiting sentencing for his sexual assault case, Dahmer again put his grandmother's basement to gruesome use: In March 1989, he lured, drugged, strangled, sodomized, photographed, dismembered and disposed of Anthony Sears, an aspiring model.

On a killing spree that lasted more than 13 years, ["Dahmer sought out men, mostly African-American, at gay bars, malls and bus stops, lured them home with promises of money or sex, and gave them alcohol laced with drugs before strangling them to death. He would then engage in sex acts with the corpses before dismembering them and disposing of them, often keeping their skulls or genitals as souvenirs."] Dahmer's darkest secret was that he was cannibalistic believing by eating part of his victims was taking their power and soul.

["He frequently took photos of his victims at various stages of the murder process, so he could recollect each act afterward and relives the experience. Dahmer was captured in 1991 and sentenced to 16 life terms. He was killed by fellow prison inmate Christopher Scarver in 1994."] However all secrets are not kept by serial killers and murders. However all secrets are not kept by serial killers and murders. Some people have secrets of abuse of power and authority. People of executive power, celebrities, and law enforcement commit illicit acts behind closed doors and use them to extort or control others who may be involved. Over the years TV celebrity, millionaire, and now President Donald Trump has a life full of secrets.

Donald Trump's obsession to be the most important person in the world has built a brand through the media that made his life the most controversial in America. Trump's exploits gives him a notoriety that have been deceiving the American people for decades. The persona Trump projects to the public covers up the secrets of his business dealings, family fortune, alleged sex abuse, domestic violence, alleged tax evasion and money laundering, racism, and other corruption that is coming to light every day. The secrets Trump hides from his childhood are still locked deep within his mind but manifested through a Narcissistic Personality that makes him try to convince people only he have all the answers and can solve all the country's problems.

However from the time Trump first made his splash into New York his goal was to become part of the elite high class social society that never accepted him. To gain influence in social and business status Trump became his own publicist creating false personas for several different personalities that would influence whoever he would be addressing at the time. Trump became a master at deception and propaganda that would become his most valued asset as time pass. Before moving to New York started taking opportunities to make his own money by investing in real estate in Brooklyn but he wanted much more, everything was never enough. Most of the family's properties were slums they intentionally rented to African Americans, immigrants and other minorities forcing segregation. Their substandard housing was rented out at extremely profitable rates with up keep or satisfactory or acceptable in quality or quantity. But also the family owned other properties they only rented to Whites at moderate rates. Eight years after the signing of Civil Rights Act in 1965 this became problem for the family when a Black woman was refused the rental of an apartment in 1973.

["The U.S. Justice Department's Civil Rights Division filed sued his father and his company in 1973 for refusing to rent apartments to black people. According to the Village Voice, the Urban League sent white and black testers to apartments owned by family company.

The white applicants received the apartments, while the blacks didn't. His father negotiated a consent decree with the DOJ, requiring him to advertise vacancies in minority papers and list them with the Urban League. The Justice Department said "racially discriminatory conduct by his father's employees and agents has occurred with such frequency that it has created a substantial impediment to the full enjoyment of equal opportunity."] This was unacceptable as far as he could see it, and he still had his sight set on having his own money crossing the river to build an empire in a high rent district with high class clientele. He would spend days sometimes weeks at a time in the city prospecting real estate deals by day and hanging out in the clubs and hot spots by night.

He would frequent night clubs where he could meet mobsters, Attorneys, bankers, business men and politicians exploiting the family name to build a reputation as a deal maker and investor. By now his father's health was failing from early signs of Alzheimer's disease, yet he still could not take control of the family's wealth. Trump's father would drive his Cadillac to one of his many construction sites after the day's work was over." "His father wearing a natty suit with his chiseled features and wide grin resembled a silent-film star." He would walk through the studs and across the plywood floors, picking up unused nails to hand back to his carpenters the next day."] Desperate to make his first business deal he was not above lying to anyone about anything.

Although his father was ill he led him to believe he needed money for an existing project and talked him into lending him over one million dollars, leaving the next day going back to the city. It would be more than a year before he went back to Brooklyn, "suffering from Alzheimer's disease his became sick with pneumonia in 1999. He died in June of that year." "According to his obituary, his father had a net worth of $250 to $300 million when he died," and also "known as a frugal man, despite his wealth." Returning to New York City and his lavished life style as a flamboyant playboy and entrepreneur he used the money he borrowed from his father as collateral to secure a line of credit. With money from his few real estate and management holding in Brooklyn and the money from his father he now had his own assets to use as he please to build his empire.

His association with mobsters, conmen and unethical attorneys, he found corruption the fastest method of accumulating vast amounts of undeclared cash. He soon mastered the business practice of using other people's money for personal gain. Many time he used false financial statement and fraudulent statements and other information to obtain bank loans more than double his net worth. In addition he manipulated and con investors into financing his investment deals so that he would never take a loss. Association with mobsters, conmen, and crooked attorneys corruption was five times more profitable than legal business operations.

Extortion, protection rackets and tax evasion was standard operation procedure. Using shell companies and buffers (several people to give orders and pass information) provided deniability and legal cover for illicit operations. Some of this was practice by his father but most learned from Italian and Russian Mafia. His father never trusted immigrants or foreigners, or that anyone should share or get rich from his work or business assets, and never joined or did business with organizations outside the family. Although up to his eyebrows in corruption his father used rational and critical thinking, and personal pride as way of survival. In addition with his father it was always a question of supremacy and segregation, ethnic groups and races should never mix.

However there was an illicit part of his life even his father never knew. Using the perception of being a rich playboy he was still molesting women. Most of his life was involved in sexually abusing, sexually assaulting, harassing and degrading women. There is no way of knowing how many women were victims of his sexual deviance, most were afraid to report it because he was rich and they believed nothing would be done. Some women blamed themselves, and some were paid for their silence. Rumors circulated around the affluent social set he had abuse and sexually assaulted more than of young ladies that were afraid to come forward in fear of embarrassment, humiliation, and destroying their reputations from retaliation and retribution.

Disrespecting women was a natural way of life as he saw it, they had no rights and men were their masters. No one ever verified the claims or proved these accusations to be true or false, or if the information started by Trump. Socially isolated trusting no one but himself, Trump has decided to be his own God and ruler placing himself above everyone without compassion. The veracity of Trump's corruption has not been exposed nor has he ever been charged with a criminal but undergoing several investigations. One investigation into Trump's secrets involves his complicity in collusion with Russia and conspiracy in hacking e-mails of Hillary Clinton during the 2016 elections. However, during this same time period Trump exposed a secret what should have been catastrophic to his winning the election.

Donald Trump has always been his own worst enemy; he never learned that the loudest person in the room is the weakest person in the room. His narcissistic personality disorder and authoritarian obsession for power, sex and wealth, and obsession for greed placed him as the center of attention at all times. He allowed himself to be videotaped bragging and boasting about sexually assaulting women. On the tape he was recorded saying he approach women and kisses them and gropes them without their permission. Because he was a celebrity he could do anything he wanted even grab them by the pussy. This was a secret Trump never thought would ever be exposed. After seeing the tape on the national news more than a dozen women came forward with accusation against him.

Chapter Three

Looking in the Closet

But also Trump's admission opened the flood gates for other women to come forward revealing heart wrenching secrets of bitter pain and embarrassment, and also the secrets and truth about other people of power and influence. Two of the men exposed in secrets of sexual misconduct were Harvey Weinstein and Bill Cosby. It appeared every man with authority was keeping secrets of sexual misconduct or harassment. Names on the list of people accused of sexual misconduct include according to Corey, D., "Harvey Weinstein allegedly sexually harassed or assaulted multiple women over decades." "Ben Affleck was accused of groping "Hilarie Burton," an "actress and former host of MTV's" "Total Request Live," in the early 2000s."

"Roy Price, the Amazon Studios chief, resigned from his job after reports surfaced of his alleged sexual misconduct toward an Amazon TV producer, and Oliver Stone." "Actress and former Playboy model Carrie Stevens accused writer and director Oliver Stone of groping her at a party during the 1990s in a tweet responding to Stone's remarks about the Harvey Weinstein scandal." The accusations and outrage continue to grow, as more women come forward with even more names and claims. Many other high profile personalities are facing troubling accusations.

["Bob Weinstein, Five days after blasting, Harvey Weinstein, as a "very sick man," himself was accused of making repeated advances to a showrunner and not accepting the word no for answer an answer."] The larger the list of sexual misconduct grew the more shadows begun to extinguish the light of moral conviction when the names of even more individuals appeared on list that people had respected for years as ["James Toback, 38 women described instances of sexual harassment from veteran Hollywood writer and director, former President George H.W. Bush, Six women from separate incidents have come forward to accuse him of touching them from behind while they posed beside him for photos." "Some said he also told them a dirty joke."] Mark Halperin after multiple reports surfaced that he sexually harassed at least a dozen women while serving as political director for ABC News."

"Kevin Spacey "House of Cards" star was accused by Broadway veteran Anthony Rapp of climbing on top of him in a sexual manner when he was 14 years old and Spacey was 26 or 27 at a party in Space's New York apartment." Each passing day it appears a culture of sexual misconduct and accused perpetrators are named by their victims. Many people in America was shocked to find out sexual abuse was so widespread. There are dozens of others accused of bring this shame to the moral standards of this country including "Dustin Hoffman, Brett Ratner, Steven Seagal, Louis C.K., and Andrew Kreisberg."

"Hollywood mogul Harvey Weinstein was fired from the studio he co-founded after a wave of employees and actresses, including Gwyneth Paltrow and Angelina Jolie alleged sexual harassment and assault in back-to-back reports. Gwyneth Paltrow and Angelina Jolie accusations were reported in "The New York Times and The New Yorker." "Asia Argento, an Italian actress reported she was sexually assaulted by Weinstein in 1997. "Asia Argento also included list of names of more than 80 women who had allegedly been sexually harassed, assaulted, raped or molested by Weinstein dating back to the late 1970s." "Argento said she compiled the list with help from other Weinstein accusers." "Time magazine has named The Silence Breakers" some of the women "who set off a national focus for sexual harassment and assault as its 2017 Person of the Year." ["The magazine said it's "unsurprising" that the year began with the women's march in Washington, D.C., and ended with women speaking out about experiences with sexual harassment and assault."

"Ashley Judd, Susan Fowler, Adama Iwu, Taylor Swift and Isabel Pascual are on the cover of the magazine and were chosen to represent hundreds of women who have broken their silence this year. Time Editor-in-Chief Edward Felsenthal called the movement, "one of the highest-velocity shifts in our culture since the 1960s."] Most of the country was giving support to the courageous women who came forward to fight a culture battle that was long overdue.

However in Alabama another story was brewing and about to cause an on slot of allegations that would include Capitol Hill. Headlines in almost every source of media lead with the story of "Judge Roy Moore Allegedly Had Sexual Encounter with Underage Girl When He Was a District Attorney." Roy Moore can be considered the worst of all child molesters and sex abusers of this century. Moore brings much more than sexual abuse, pedophilia, and extreme racism from a life of dark existence. Roy Moore a former assistant District Attorney, Judge, politician and community leader has no respect for the laws of this country. Judge Roy Moore twice removed from the bench for failing to obey and up hold the laws. One of Moore's acts of misconduct was ordering the violation of the laws by public officials on same sex marriage and marriage equality.

Moore's second offense was pertaining to ordering the statue of the Ten Commandments not be removed from the court. Moore displayed his racism not wanting to allow Muslims to hold a senate seat. Roy Moore is an authority figure that makes life altering decisions over people's lives with extreme bias. Roy Moore's resume is tainted with illicit acts the people cannot trust, not even other Republicans. According to Mystal, E., ["Judge Roy Moore, currently running to be God's voice in the United States Senate, has been accused of having a" "sexual encounter" "with a 14-year-old girl when he was a 32-year-old assistant District attorney in 1979."

"The Washington Post reports that three other women allege that Moore" "pursued" "them when they were between 16 and 18 and Moore was in his"] Allegations against Roy Moore states Moore was ["an officer of the court creating private time with a 14-year-old girl at court and then later, allegedly, groping her." "Disgusting as it" may be Moore "tried to get" "ahead" "of the story by going to Breitbart News" denying the "allegations. Breitbart does the work of suggesting this is" a "fake news plot against Moore lead by Jeff Bezos's Washington Post." It appears only Breitbart readers and deplorable people will accept "pedophilia is something fundamentally cool" as "long as it's done in Jesus' name."] Many people who are not "Breitbart readers won't drill down in the story because if you keep going the Alt-Right defense of Moore becomes stranger and grosser." Mystal, E., also stated in another "Post interviewed four women who claimed that Moore engaged in inappropriate behavior; Moore's denial is limited to the" "allegations" "and doesn't get into the specificity of the things the various women talk about in the Post's story."

Roy Moore is "focused on the lead woman who is the only one alleging a" "sexual" "encounter." Roy Moore will do great harm to his state and the country just as he has to his victims if elected as a United States Senator, yet he won't drop out the race. Moore refuses to accept responsibility or show any remorse for his misconduct. Just like with other Personalities recently accused of sexual misconduct, Moore continues to lie, deny, and lie some more.

Even with most of the Senate democrats and republicans pushing for Moore to quit, why should he? Moore is not the only one who will be on Capitol Hill with "allegations" of sexual misconduct. Two United States Senators introduced new legislation on sexual misconduct in congress. According to Zaman, A. ["At a House hearing on how to prevent sexual abuse female members of Congress shared their experiences of sexual misconduct involving lawmakers." "Rep. Jackie Speier told the panel two current House members, a Republican and a Democrat, engaged in sexual harassment."] ["In fact, there are two members of Congress, Republican and Democrat, now serving, who has been subject to review.

However both but have engaged in sexual harassment" and "propositions such as 'Are you going to be a good girl?' to perpetrators exposing their genitals, to victims having their private parts grabbed on the House floor." Speier added, "We do know that about $15 million has been paid out by the House on behalf of harassers in the last 10 to 15 years."] Roy Moore and other like him with personality disorders believe they are above the law. Moore is only following other demons of the dark; Donald Trump was elected with an even worst past. The morals, illegal activities, pedophilia, and extreme racism mean nothing to White supremacist as long as they believe they are in control of the country.

Some others in the country and Alabama don't understand the harsh implications and examples it would give other pedophiles and predators. Most members of the Republican Party see it as political and holding on to governing legislation. This is not just the opinion of one; it appears the majority of America really has the same opinion. All of those who oppose the evidence, facts and truth have in one thing in common, they all supporters of the Alt-right and ignore the dark times and places in American history. However the people are beginning to reject the lies and deceit that has taken over the political world. Culture has become more of a major issue in politics as Stock Markets and deficits. Although money is important to living in America, the way of life has more value.

The Me Too Movement, Women's Rights protest groups, Africans and Hispanics all came together for one cause. The protest had slowed to a crawl as the country was focused on Bill Cosby and the outcome of his trail. According to prosecutors ["Bill Cosby was able to hide his crimes for decades behind his fame and fortune, Montgomery County District Attorney Kevin Steele said at a press conference following the sentencing. The comedian once known as America's Dad was especially able to hide behind wholesome character on "The Cosby Show," Dr. Cliff Huxtable, Steele said. "It was a seminal character on TV, and so was the family, but it was fiction," Steele said."] CNN reported ["Bill Cosby was processed at the Montgomery Correctional Facility in Eagleville, Pennsylvania after being sentenced to 3-10 years in a state prison. He was also fined $25,000 plus the costs of prosecution."]

["Not long after, Cosby was then moved to State Correctional Institution at Phoenix, a state prison, for diagnostic and intake. There, his needs and health issues will be evaluated as officials decide which prison best suits him overall."] Much of the country was excited or shocked into dismay over the Cosby verdict, while congress was trying to get by with confirming a Supreme Court Justice with a thirty si6 year old skeleton in is closet. Judge Brett Kavanaugh nominee to the Supreme Court appear to have secrets from his high school and college years. During confirmation hearings the closet door opened and there were many secrets lurking in the dark for over thirty five years. Deborah Ramirez, Christine Blasey Ford and Julie Swetnick are three women making accusations unethical, ill moral and possible sexual abuse or harassment against Kavanaugh. According to Chokshi and Jacobs of the New York Times "Dr. Blasey was the first to accuse Judge Kavanaugh, but she was not alone. Two other women have come forward publicly in recent days with allegations against him, while an additional anonymous accusation surfaced on Wednesday."

During "the hearing, Dr. Blasey came across as an Everywoman with a Ph.D. Her testimony was a stark reminder of gender dynamics and of the mental gymnastics required of women who speak up." The other two women did not testify at the hearing however there accusations came out in the media. Deborah Ramirez accused Judge Kavanaugh of exposing himself to her at a drunken college party.

However her accusations are under investigation, at the time of the accusations there was no evidence to support her claim. Julie Swetnick stated "Judge Kavanaugh was "present" when she was raped at a high school party." Her accusations were not verified at the time either, however because of other information that appears to be true prompted a more extensive investigation and a delay in conformation process. Judge Kavanaugh did more harm to himself exposing secrets by lying under oath. Judge Kavanaugh misrepresented the facts on stolen e-mails during his first confirmation hearing. But also the most damaging secrets were exposed when Kavanaugh continued to lie and deny his consumption of alcohol during high school, college, and his first years working in Washington. Once accusations were made about Kavanaugh's drinking problems, classmates, ex-roommates, police reports, and most damaging hand written letters by Kavanaugh begun to surface as evidence collaborating the allegations.

In addition Kavanaugh's demeanor, attitude, temperament and political bias unfitting for a Judge of any level showed with extreme prejudice. Kavanaugh's words and actions asserts contempt for equality and fairness, but also shows he is hiding secrets detrimental to society and culture in America. Kavanaugh's or the Supreme Court's future are not set. An investigation into the book of Kavanaugh is still open and nothing has been decided. The American people must come to their senses and search for the answers to two questions, if Kavanaugh is innocent what is he hiding? Also why lie?

Chapter Four

Religious Sex Secrets

Kavanaugh still hides dark secrets stating "what happens at Georgetown Prep, says at Georgetown Prep. History has taught the American people that everyone holds a secret and anyone's secret can have illicit motives.

Everyone places their trust and faith in their religious beliefs and leadership. The most highly trusted and respected members of any community are the Pastors, Preachers, Ministers and Priest.

All members of the church from the Pope to the deacon are held to the highest ethical and moral standards, and considered to be of impeccable integrity. For many years the Catholic Church has been keeping many dark and sometimes deadly sex secrets. For decades The Catholic Church has quietly addressed allegations of sexual abuse. One of the best kept secrets has been the over 1000 cases of sexual abuse within the Catholic Church. Most cases of sex abuse or child rape were taken care of within the church under confidentiality as isolated incidents. With little to no publicity the church would allow time to cover up and hide the offenses from the eyes of the public without really solving the problem. According to Park, M. of CNN "For more than three decades, the Catholic Church has been rocked by sex abuse scandals spanning the globe."["

And for decades, the church has been accused of protecting itself rather than the victims of child sexual abuse. Here are some major scandals and revelations involving the Catholic Church and allegations of abuse."] In 2017 ["Cardinal George Pell, a senior adviser to Pope Francis and the third-ranking official in the Holy See, is taking leave from the Vatican to fight historical sexual assault charges in his home country of Australia. The case is the latest black mark against the Catholic Church, which has been reeling from sexual abuse scandals across several countries that date back decades. It could also have ramifications for Pope Francis, who counts Pell among his closest aides.

Australian police have not released a detailed list of charges against Pell and didn't disclose any information about alleged victims, saying only that there were multiple charges and "multiple complainants."] The secrets of Cardinal George Pell came to light about three years after the exposure of Jozef Wesolowski. "In 2014 Jozef Wesolowski, a former Vatican ambassador to the Dominican Republic was found guilty of sexual abuse of minors by a Vatican tribunal and defrocked in 2014." ["He was accused of sexual abuse of minors and possession of child pornography during his time as papal nuncio to the Dominican Republic. Italy's Corriero Della Sera reported that Wesolowski's laptop contained more than 100,000 files with pornographic images and videos. Wesolowski's was the highest-ranking Catholic official arrested for alleged sexual abuse of minors. He died in 2015, before he could be put on trial."]

Even as Jozef Wesolowski was on trial, the Catholic Church was aware of other incidence and allegations of sexual misconduct within the church."2011 Thousands of children suffered from sexual abuse in the Dutch Roman Catholic Church over more than six decades, and about 800 "possible perpetrators" have been identified, according to an independent Commission of Inquiry, issued in 2011." "The Commission of Inquiry said it received 1,795 reports of church-related sex abuse of minors; "reports contained information about possible perpetrators." "2010 Allegations of sexual abuse spread across more than a half dozen countries.

Some of these countries included Austria, Germany, the Netherlands, Spain, Switzerland and Brazil, home of the world's largest Catholic population." Revelations about church abuse included the Munich, Germany, archdiocese where Pope Benedict XVI once served as archbishop. Under the Pope's tenure as archbishop in the early 1980s, the Munich archdiocese ignored warnings to keep a molesting priest away from children, said the doctor, Werner Huth, who issued those warnings. Huth demanded the priest, Rev. Peter Hullermann never be allowed to interact with children again. Instead, the church allowed the priest to return to work and to deal with children. Hullermann was convicted of abusing minors in 1986. Pope Benedict had left the Munich archdiocese for a new post in 1982"] Even with ongoing allegations and incidents the church maintained public silence never addressing questions of ongoing investigations.

However there were earlier reports that were neither confirmed nor denied. In 2009 ["a bombshell report commissioned by the Irish government concluded that the Archdiocese of Dublin and other Catholic Church authorities in Ireland covered up clerical child abuse. The Dublin Archdiocese Commission of Investigation's 720-page report said that it has "no doubt that clerical child sexual abuse was covered up" from January 1975 to May 2004, the time covered by the report. The commission had been set up in 2006 to look into allegations of child sexual abuse made against clergy in the Irish capital.

The report named 11 priests who had pleaded guilty to or were convicted of sexual assaults on children. Of the other 35, it gave pseudonyms to 33 of them and redacted the names of two."] The information and secrets that follows go way beyond one writer's research and Efforts, but the dedication and work of a collective of investigators and reporters from around the world and across the country. However the findings are so shocking the stories must be told with as much accuracy, truth and factual evidence possible

. ["In recent months, USA TODAY Network reporters at the Pacific Daily News have uncovered scores of allegations involving 14 Catholic priests on Guam, where a former altar boy's accusation last summer that Archbishop Anthony Apuron sexually abused him in the 1970s has prompted other revelations."] It has been reported abuse cases have roiled Catholic parishes elsewhere the nation, many times decades after evidence of the illicit assaults surfaced. ["The O'Brien case, an Arizona man sued, claiming repressed memories resurfaced two years ago, according to court documents. The lawsuit accuses O'Brien, now 81, of sexual abuse from 1977 through 1982. O'Brien, who stepped aside as an active bishop in June 2003 after he was found guilty of leaving the scene of a fatal accident, denies the accusation. The suit names 60 other Roman Catholic priests or church employees, dating back to the 1950s and alleges a cover-up."]

The Catholic diocese eventually exposed number priests as connected to an agreement with Arizona prosecutors in the 2000s, whereas two of the priests fled the U.S. and remain at large and a much larger number were dead. "A Maricopa County Superior Court judge is considering diocese attorneys' motions to dismiss several of the lawsuit's 14 claims." An agreement in 2003 during O'Brien's case asserted important alterations "within the Catholic Church in the Phoenix area, including victim assistance and training on sexual misconduct for all diocesan staff and volunteers."

A number of "accusations of sex crimes involving Catholic priests and children in Louisiana may date back seven decades, court record showed." Court records also show, in "the case of Rev. F. David Broussard, who is expected in St. Martin Parish court on the 27th of November, is most recent." "The former pastor in Breaux Bridge, La., who was accused of sexual contact with children, was charged with 500 counts of child pornography after investigators say they found hundreds of images in his personal computer." Also "former priest Mark A. Broussard (no relation to F. David Broussard), was convicted in 2016 of molesting altar boys in the neighboring diocese of Lake Charles during the 1980s, was arrested in 2012 after a man wrote to Lake Charles Bishop Glen John Provost to make accusations against him."]

"Mark Broussard was sentenced to two consecutive life sentences for aggravated rape and 50 additional years for sexual abuse. The Lafayette-area cases were just two of many involving local priests and children." "Minnesota Public Radio investigation uncovered a wealth of court-related documents tied to such incidents in the Diocese of Lafayette in 2014." "Rev. Harry Flynn, a bishop in both Lafayette and Minnesota, where sex abuse cases involving the clergy uncovered cases revealing more than 14 Lafayette priests were involved in sexually abusing children." "The accused served in myriad church positions across the Lafayette diocese, including in small Acadiana towns as Abbeville, where Gauthe's case drew nationwide attention.

Gauthe admitted to raping or sodomizing 37 children dating back to 1972. In 1986, he pleaded guilty to 11 counts of child molestation and was sentenced to 20 years in prison, but he was released a decade early when many as 100 people may have been abused by Gauthe, according to a watchdog website. The Catholic Church's response today to accusations of sex abuse involving clergy members is much different than it was in the latter half of the 20th century. When priests are merely be reassigned to different parishes, evidence shows the guilt." "Bishop Provost turned over accusations against Mark Broussard to police; Bishop Deshotel cooperated with local authorities when F. David Broussard was arrested." In addition "the Diocese of Lafayette says it marches in step with the Catholic Church's mandates to protect children and since 2003 has enacted practices including criminal background checks and fingerprinting for clergy who have contact with minors."

"In 2002, as a child sexual abuse scandal in Boston's archdiocese engulfed the Catholic Church, The News Journal in Wilmington, Del., began chronicling decades of child abuse, cover-ups and quiet transfers of priests from one parish to another." By 2011, the Diocese of Wilmington and several religious orders throughout the diocese distributed more than $110 million to 152 adult survivors who were sexually abused by area Catholic priests." Large settlements kept the incidents confidential and behind closed doors. The victims were now complicit in keeping the secret of sex abuse in the Church.

"Tens of millions more were paid in confidential settlements with dozens of other childhood rape survivors who had been abused in families, other churches, non-profit groups or in public, private or religious schools in Delaware according to reports from "TheNews Journal."] It is very baffling to conceive how so many incidents of sexual misconduct can be hidden from the public for such a long period of time by one organization such as the Catholic Church. Dozens of living and deceased priests were exposed as abusers.

However these were not the only cases reported, other cases were reported in Minnesota, New York, California, Pennsylvania, and Iowa. What is more disturbing is the Catholic Church is not the only religious organization that pastor, preachers and other clergy facing allegations or charges of sex abuse or rape of minor children. Many people are not aware of the 2001 movie Spotlight that told the account of child molestation and cover up in the Catholic Church until the Boston Globe story was nominated for an Oscar. However shining a light on the dark secrets of the Catholic Church brought attention to other religious organizations. Baptist author raises the argument with factual evidence in her book that clergy secrets of sexual abuse aren't just a Catholic problem. According to Allen, B. ["Author Jeri Massi says abuse victims have been written off, discarded and even vilified in the pulpits of both Independent Baptists and the Southern Baptist Convention.

Her The Big Book of Bad Baptist Preachers catalogues 100 cases of preachers and churches involved in child molestation scandals in the last 20 years."] Massi states in the introduction of her book "sexual abuse of children is part and parcel of the cultures of the Independent Baptists and Southern Baptists." Most people find it hard to accept, many just do not believe there are monsters inside their Church. Baptist Church leadership appears to ignore rumors and private allegations. However Massi writes "when confronted by the scale of the problem, Baptist leadership has "at best turned a deaf ear.

Addressing victims who encountered the assault at worst has countered with threats and intimidation." It is also chronicled in Messi's book ["abuse victims and their advocates are routinely accused of "painting with a broad brush." In her own Independent Fundamental Baptist tradition, she says she has been depicted as sexually promiscuous, a drug addict and a witch and had her life threatened three times."]

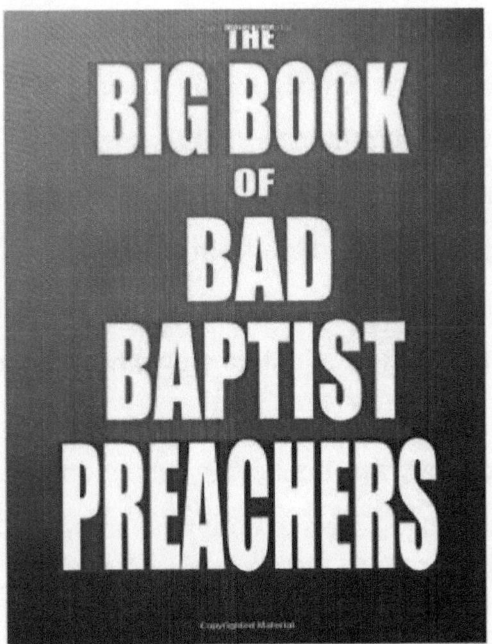

Whistleblowers don't fare much better in the Southern Baptist Convention, she says, quoting SBC leaders denouncing the advocacy group Survivors Network of those Abused by Priests as "opportunists motivated by personal gain" and "just as reprehensible as sex criminals."

Because of whistleblowers and victim beginning to come forward contrary to the arguments posed by many church leaders, the problem of clergy sex abuse of children in conservative Baptist churches is on a very large scale, and doesn't appear to be diminishing. Also it seems as if "Baptist leaders were reluctant to implement measures safeguarding congregations as receiving and compiling abuse reports so offenders cannot remain in or re-enter the ministry." It was stated by Massi "many churches embrace a dangerous fallacy that simply firing a pastor is a remedy for sin, instead of relying on the legal system to weed out criminals. This is suggesting "Baptist Church leaders have moral responsibility to eradicate sexual predators that are never prosecuted and free to roam from church to church." It was not hard for the world to see this was just a method of pushing back on the publicity hiding the truth from public view knowing people would forget over time.

Society have a way of believing if they don't see something or hear it, then everything's fine and nothing is threating their peace of mind. However that peace of mind never came as more sexual assaults were being reported involving members of the clergy inside Baptist and Evangelist Church. Media stories of sexual assaults and child rape begun to surface all across the country. Hill, C. reported ["A Rockingham County North Carolina pastor and principal is facing charged for sex crimes involving a minor. Kevin "Scott" Heffner has been arrested for 14 counts of sex crimes involving a minor.

Heffner is the pastor at Victory Baptist Church and the principal at Victory Baptist Academy. He is at the Rockingham Detention Center under a $1 million bond. Kevin "Scott" Heffner, 48, is the pastor of Victory Baptist Church and the principal of Victory Baptist Academy in Ruffin. He has been charged with twelve counts of disseminating obscene materials to a minor and two counts of statutory sex offense. Heffner was placed in the Rockingham County Detention Center under a $1 million secured bond and is scheduled to appear in court on Sept. 9th. A former Abilene church daycare worker accused of child sex crimes was released Wednesday after a judge reduced his bond by $250,000."] Benjamin Russell Roberts, 23, of Abilene Texas was ["charged with indecency with a child and continuous sexual abuse of a child, was being held on $350,000 bond. Judge Thomas Wheeler reduced it to $100,000. Roberts will not be allowed to have access to the internet or a phone and he will have to wear a GPS monitoring device.

Roberts was arrested in March. He worked at Wylie Baptist's CDC and childcare programs at two other Abilene churches. Police originally discovered Roberts after a child pornography investigation led them to his address in north Abilene. According to court documents, Roberts admitted that a child from his neighborhood slept over at his house and at one point they were together in the same bed "spooning."

The child told police that he spent the night at Roberts' house on more than one occasion and also stated that he would never go into Roberts' room because he was "afraid of getting raped." The child reportedly "shut down" when he was asked why he was afraid of being raped."]"On March 28, Roberts admitted to police that he downloaded child pornography and had "sexual thoughts of the children with whom he worked." "Roberts also admitted that he became sexually aroused by one child. "Another incident reported surfaced involving a ["former youth pastor at a Conway church faces numerous charges of sex crimes against two young girls after they revealed the abuse that happened four years ago, according to a report from Horry County police. Officers responded to Langston Baptist Church, located at 763 Highway 905, on June 27 to speak with the pastor who revealed allegations made against a youth pastor of the church. The pastor informed officers that two girls who attend the church told him they were sexually assaulted by Norman Abernathy, 58, of Conway, four to five years ago.

Abernathy most recently served as the youth pastor at Langston Baptist Church, but resigned from the position following the allegations, the report states. While Abernathy was not on staff at the church during the alleged abuse, he was "an active member" of the church, the pastor confirms. The victims, who are now adults, were friends with Abernathy's step-daughter and were often at his home.

According to the pastor, the victims told him Abernathy would put his hands down their pants, grab their breasts, and pull them onto his lap."] Although ["when the pastor confronted Abernathy, the suspect denied the allegations, the report states. A July 11 interview with one victim revealed the girl was in 7th or 8th grade and was spending time in Abernathy's home to visit his stepdaughter. She was lying in a hammock in the backyard when Abernathy approached her, put his hand down her shirt and under her bra and then made her promise not to tell anyone, according to the police report. The victim says she told her parents and when Abernathy was confronted, he denied doing anything wrong, claiming it was an accident."] There is an epidemic of denial about sexual abuse in the Baptist Church and the Evangelical church. Across the United States, evangelical churches are failing to protect victims of sexual abuse among their members.

["The MeToo movement has swept into communities of faith, several high-profile leaders have fallen: Paige Patterson, the president of Southwestern Baptist Theological Seminary, was forced into early retirement this month after reports that he'd told a rape victim to forgive her assailant rather than call the police. Illinois megachurch pastor Bill Hybels similarly retired early after several women said he'd dispensed lewd comments, unwanted kisses and invitations to hotel rooms."]There are so many people torn between their faith and convictions for the church, justice for the victims, and the lives of the Accused offenders, some things are kept secret and hidden in time.

The victims are hurt the most physically and mentally carrying emotional and sometimes mental scars and secrets for life. He offenders many times slip away carrying their secrets to other locations and continue to destroy lives, while just a few go to prison. But how much loss is it for the church organizations? ["So many Christian churches in the United States do so much good nourishing the soul, comforting the sick, providing services, counseling congregants, teaching Jesus's example, and even working to fight sexual abuse and harassment. But like in any community of faith, there is also sin often silenced, ignored and denied, and it is much more common than many want to believe. It has often led to failures by evangelicals to report sexual abuse, respond appropriately to victims and change the institutional cultures that enabled the abuse in the first place."] However society must remember it is more than the religious leadership keeping secrets and protecting themselves from bad publicity and financial loss. All the sexual predators, pedophiles, rapist and sexual deviants exclusive belong to the church.

It is many other people out there with dark illicit secrets of bad sexual behavior, or social mental disorders children are exposed to every day. Most parents can't spend every hour of the day physically holding our children's hands protecting them from the crazies and the evils in life. People must also provide for our families, educate our children, and take responsibility for the overall care of the members who cannot care for themselves.

Chapter Five

School System Predators

Daily living requires a person to share their lives with others, which means others will play a part in their lives. Learning institutions had been the safest place people could send their children each day without worry or threat of harm. School systems provided more than a formal education. Schools provided safety, physical fitness, discipline, citizenship, pride in accomplishment and self-esteem. Recent safety issues are top concern in schools now because of bullying, gang activity and drugs in some areas, and the rash of school shootings across the country. Society still look to the teachers, coaches, councilors and school staff and facility they believe have the morals, values, and integrity, with the commitment and dedication to continue to do their job. State and local governments search for people with all of these virtues through background checks that uncover everything except their darkest secrets. More than just isolated incidents sexual deviants and child abusers are within the school systems.

Many stories don't get media attention because of stories and events of national attention that are believed to be much larger stories, with a much greater importance. However searching media archives there are stories and reports of crimes the never knew were committed. News media across the country gives accounts of sexual misconduct by teachers or affiliated school staff as coaches, trainers, doctors or aids.

According to "Legal Information" provided by "LawFirms" "Teacher Sex Offender List: 25 Female Teacher and Student Sex Crime Scandals." Five of the cases included list ["Melissa Ann Andreini was a special education educator at Helper Junior High School in Helper, Utah when she came under investigation for sexual relations with a fifteen-year-old male student at her school. According to the criminal complaint, Andreini paid the student $1,500 after having sex with her in her home, which she later admitted. Criminal charges filed against Andreini include three counts of third degree felony unlawful sexual activity with a minor."] ["Keri Ann Brekne was a seventh grade teacher in the social studies department at Lopatcong Township Middle School located in Phillipsburg, New Jersey when she was arrested for sexual assault against a fourteen-year-old girl in both her home in Bethlehem, Pennsylvania, as well as in the female child's home in New Jersey."]

["Brekne has pled guilty to charges in both states. Criminal charges filed against Andreini include three counts of third degree felony unlawful sexual activity with a minor. Lisa Lynette Clark was a thirty-seven (37) year old mother, who attempted to marry a fifteen-year-old male, who happened to be a friend of her son, under a bizarre legal loophole under Georgia law. Clark and the victim attempted to marry under a Georgia law stating that underage individuals may marry if the bride at the time is expecting child."]

[" Criminal charges against Clark included one count of statutory rape through plea bargaining, which led Clark to serve a nine month period of incarceration with probation and other community control restrictions to follow her release. Under a plea agreement, Clark has agreed to serve a nine (9) month sentence for pleading guilty to statutory rape, including agreeing not to communicate with the victim, or her husband, until he turns seventeen (17) years old. Additionally, Clark is now registered as a lifelong sex offender and is not allowed contact with any children aside from her own."]

["Margaret De Barracuda, then age 30 at the time of the crime, was an interim teacher at McClatchy High School in Sacramento, California when police officers found her and a sixteen (16) year old male student behind the school in a parked car. Investigators learned that the male student had actually seduced Barraicua over time, and finally, the woman gave into the underage student's sexual advances, which lead to the incident behind the high school."]

"Criminal charges against Barraicua eventually became four counts of statutory rape, which she was forced to serve one year imprisonment." "Geisel a 42-year old teacher employed at Christian Brothers Academy in Albany, N.Y when allegations and criminal charges arose surrounding sexual conduct with multiple male students. Geisel was noted for having sexual relations with three students. Geisel claims the latter two students were involved with her sexually against her will due to their attempts to blackmail the woman."

[“Criminal charges against Geisel initially were two felony counts of rape in the third degree and two counts of endangering the welfare of a minor, but through plea bargaining, Geisel and her attorney were able to greatly reduce the severity and number of actual charges she pled guilty to in the end.”] [“Debra Beasley LaFave was a 23-year-old teacher at Angelo L. Greco Middle School in Temple Terrace, Florida when she was arrested for having multiple sex encounters with a fourteen-year-old student throughout various locations in the school, including performing oral sex on the male student in her classroom and having intercourse with him in a portable classroom located on the school campus.”] “Criminal Charges of two counts of lewd and lascivious battery in exchange for pleading guilty are those applied in the case, which allowed LaFave to avoid jail time.”

Lisa Lavoie a twenty-four year old teacher at Maurice A. Donahue Elementary School located in Holyoke, Massachusetts when charged with six counts of statutory rape, three counts of aggravated rape and abuse, and three counts of statutory rape, and enticement of a minor regarding a fifteen-year-old male student. After the boy’s parents alerted authorities regarding their son’s possible relationship with the teacher, Lavoie and the underage boy went on the lam travelling up and down the east coast of the U.S. Criminal charges against Lavoie include six counts of statutory rape, three counts of aggravated rape and abuse, and three counts of statutory rape.

In addition to charges of enticement, however, no ruling on any of the charges has been made at the time. According to Miltimore, J. ["In Texas, home to the largest number of teacher sexual misconduct cases in the country, investigations into alleged inappropriate teacher-student relationships has grown 27 percent over the past three years, to 179. Kentucky schools reported more than 45 sexual relationships between teachers and students in 2011, up from 25 just a year earlier. And a surge has been reported in Alabama, where the state investigated 31 cases during the year ending July 2013, nearly triple the number it had investigated just four years earlier."] Many times female sex offenses are forgotten over time, but that does not make them less harmful to society. That does not protect innocence or the emotional and mental damage of the victims.

All sex crimes are atrocious and all minors and people engaged without legal permission are victims. However some sex crimes are extremely more serious than others. A report from the Pima County Attorney's Office in Tucson AZ stated Joseph Massey, a former charter school teacher, has been convicted of luring a minor for sexual exploitation and assault, and three counts of assault for the purpose of gratification. In just one month of working at the school, Massey targeted three female students, ages 15, 15, and 18. ["The Pima County Attorney's Office says Massey would go to the students' desks, and inappropriately touch them on the thigh and buttocks while pretending to help them with their classwork.

Another student confirmed seeing the inappropriate touching of one of the victims in the classroom. Massey also offered to exchange sexual favors with one of the 15-year-old victims."] Massey was arrested in January 2016 and his sentencing is set for January 16, 2018. This is after other incidents where Massey had been arrested in 2009 for sexual misconduct with a minor and was tried and acquitted in 2010 to continue his sexual deviance. GULFPORT, Miss. (AP) "A former teacher is charged with transportation of minors with intent to engage in sexual activity." "A criminal complaint and an affidavit from an FBI agent allege there were eight victims all students at Bayou View Junior High School in Gulfport and the incidents occurred between 1973 and 1985." ["William Richard Pryor appeared in U.S. District Court in Gulfport. Pryor was turned over to U.S. marshals to be held until a preliminary and detention hearing.

["U.S. Attorney Gregory K. Davis said in a news release that Pryor traveled with the eight victims, ages 13 and 14, out of state with the intent of engaging in sexual activity. In an affidavit accompanying the criminal complaint, FBI agent Matthew Campbell says Pryor confessed to the incidents."] Camden County, Mo. two men were sentenced to 10 and 14 years in prison on multiple counts of sex crimes against children. Judge Kenneth Hayden sentenced Dustin Reed Thomas and Gary D. Morton at the Camden County Courthouse on Monday: Thomas had pleaded guilty while Morton had opted for a bench trial."]

["Thomas had entered an open guilty plea on three felony counts 2nd Degree Statutory Rape, 2nd Degree Statutory Sodomy, and 4th Degree Child Molestation. He will spend 14 years in prison, without parole. Morton was found guilty on March 8, 2018, and on Monday, April 24, Judge Hayden sentenced him to 20 years in prison, without parole. Dustin Thomas faced Judge Kenneth Hayden in Camden County Circuit Court on April 23, 2018 for a sentencing hearing. On March 7, 2018, Thomas had waived arraignment and entered an open plea of guilty to all three counts in one case, Statutory Rape-2nd Degree, Statutory Sodomy-2nd Degree, and Child Molestation-4th Degree-Child less than 17 years of age and offender greater than 4 years older."] Male sexual assaults are more violent and devastating than sex crimes committed by females, but also receive much more punishment. No amount of punishment male or female offenders may receive is not enough to amount to the life time of harm they have done to their victims.

Over time offenders punishment will end, but the victims and their families will suffer from their secrets for the rest of their lives. The only way to bring justice to society is to expose the secrets of those who are doing harm to society. However how can all the secrets become exposed when some of the people trusted to expose the secrets are the very ones hiding illicit secrets of their own? Society looks to law enforcement and medical professionals for the answers, but can they really be trusted?

Chapter Six

Law Enforcement Secrets

Nella Larsen once stated ["The freedom from violence citizenship guarantees is in fact a freedom with violence." "The protection from violence the people rely on is the assertion of violence against them."] This argument put hate, violence and secrets into the hands of politicians and law enforcement that have dark illicit secrets hiding within their organizations. Who will investigate the investigators or punish the punishers? More than sexual misconduct secrets are kept hidden. In addition to sex offenses law enforcement personnel have been involved in many criminal acts and victim of many unlawful accusations. In the past few years citizens have lost trust in law enforcement and police agencies public and private. Many people argue the breakdown in communications and distrust of police and law enforcement is a product of racial division and prejudice.

But some evidence point to something much more sinister and dangerous. Police and law enforcement from the streets to the prosecutor's office see themselves as brothers of one color (Blue). Law enforcement personnel of all agencies work closely together and closely with the court systems. Police support police and law enforcement above anything else, they work together, recreation together, and bond together. Many people define the relationship of law enforcement as a subculture that only gets closer within Precinct and Departments.

Police subculture is a distinctive set of beliefs, values, attitudes and behaviors that are shared amongst the majority of officers working in police organizations. In the view of the FBI, most officers learn and become a part of this subculture during the early part of their careers. From the time a young officer enters the academy there appears to be a secret society that influences them to believe there are two kinds of citizens, the police and everyone else. This belief and attitude has created a great divide posing threats for the public and police, what appear to be us against them society that is detrimental to all communities. Over the past few years citizens have tried to make sense of police violence that appear to be on the rise across America. Many people still use over policing, stereotyping and racial profiling in high crime neighborhoods as a reason for some police officers to use excessive force, or abuse the powers of the uniform and the attitude and behavior of the police. Even if the facts prove these things to be true very few police officers are charged and prosecuted.

Out of the number of officers that may be prosecuted and go to trial even less are convicted and punished. What happens within a prescient or department, stays in that prescient or department, Police don't testify against police. According to a research study by Professor Philip Stinson of Bowling Green State University in Ohio, ["there are more than 1,000 police shootings each year in America. Since 2005 Stinson started keeping record of shootings, over 33% of the officers were convicted for fatal on-duty shootings.

The rest were pending trial or not convicted."] Even with use of body cameras and viral videos and widespread concern over fatal shootings of unarmed black men in the United States, convictions of cops have been rare including high-profile cases. One case reigniting debates because of the lack of convictions of police shootings, particularly involving African Americans, a white former St. Louis police officer was acquitted of murder in the deadly shooting of a black man. ["Circuit Judge Timothy Wilson found Jason Stockley not guilty on charges of first-degree murder and armed criminal action. Stockley was charged more than four years after the 2011 shooting death of Anthony Lamar Smith. Stockley acquittal sparked violent protests in St. Louis.

Another fatal shooting ["28 year old Akai Gurley at a New York housing project, police officer Peter Liang claimed it was an accidental discharge. Liang, who had been on the job for 18 months, was on patrol in a dark stairwell of the building in November 2014 when he fired his gun. The bullet deflected off a wall and struck the victim in the chest. Liang was fired from the New York Police Department, was found guilty of manslaughter and official misconduct on Feb. 11, 2016, but supporters claim the officer was singled out for prosecution as a Chinese-American."] ["A judge later reduced the jury's conviction to criminally negligent homicide and sentenced Liang to five years' probation and 800 hours of community service. Some officers were never charged."]

["Eric Garner, a 43-year-old black man, died after being tackled to the ground and held in a chokehold by New York police officers for allegedly selling cigarettes illegally. Garner, who has asthma, said "I can't breathe" as the incident was captured on cellphone video. He died later that day on July 17, 2014."] ["A grand jury decided not to indict Officer Daniel Pantaleo in December 2014 and the city settled with Garner's estate for $5.9 million. Pantaleo was placed on modified duty at the New York Police Department after Garner's death. Unarmed 18-year-old Michael Brown was fatally shot by police officer Darren Wilson after a struggle in Ferguson, Mo. He was shot 12 times. A grand jury decided not to indict Wilson on Nov. 24, 2014, sparking angry protests. After a grand jury cleared Wilson, he wanted to rejoin Ferguson's police force but was told that might put other officers at risk."]

However in another city "12-year-old Tamir Rice of Cleveland was shot by a police officer while carrying an air pistol." ["Officer, Timothy Loehmann, was responding to a 911 call claiming a person was pointing "a pistol" at people. Loehmann, an officer in training, shot Rice within moments of arriving at the scene. A grand jury decided not to indict Loehmann and another officer, Frank Garmback, on Dec. 28, 2015. Administrative charges have been filed against three officers this year. Loehmann was fired by the city of Cleveland in May. The city cited alleged misinformation on his employment application to the Police Department, not his conduct in the shooting."]

Yet still in another part of the country ["37-year-old Alton Sterling was fatally shot after being pinned to the ground by officers outside a Baton Rouge convenience store. Police said he was reaching for a gun. Federal prosecutors announced in May that there isn't enough evidence to warrant civil rights charges against officers Blane Salamoni and Howie Lake II. State charges are possible. They are on paid leave from the police department."] A number of officers were acquitted or the charges dropped as in the case of "Caesar Goodson Jr., Brian W. Rice, William Porter, Alicia D. White, Garrett E. Miller, and Edward M. Nero."] An African American male ["Freddie Gray, 25, was arrested by Baltimore police after he was found with a knife in his pocket. Gray died after suffering a neck injury while in police custody. On May 21, 2015, a Baltimore grand jury indicted six police officers on charges including involuntary manslaughter and reckless endangerment."]

"Three were found not guilty by Judge Barry Williams; the other three had their charges dropped on July 27." "The Gray family and the city of Baltimore reached a $6.4 million civil settlement in September." ["Betty Jo Shelby, 43, says she was driving to another police call on Sept. 16 when she came upon Terence Crutcher, standing alongside the road. She said she then saw an SUV straddling the center line with its engine running and doors open. Graphic videos show Crutcher, 40, walking toward his SUV with his hands up and his back to multiple officers."]

["Crutcher appears to place his hands on his vehicle when he falls to the ground, shocked with a stun gun fired by one officer and shot by Shelby. Shelby was acquitted on May 17 of a first-degree manslaughter charge. The police department reinstated her after the verdict, putting her back on the force."] ["50-year-old Walter Scott, driving with a broken brake light, was shot while running from North Charleston police officer Michael Slager. The officer, who was fired from the police force, was charged with first-degree murder after a cellphone video was released. A mistrial was declared in 2016. Last month, Slager pleaded guilty to a federal charge of using excessive force. State murder charges against Slager were dismissed as part of the plea deal."] Case after case there is almost the same outcome, police go free. Grand Jurys are held in secret with a city, county, or state prosecutor presenting the case. Information given to Grand Jurys is confidential, only the prosecutor controls what evidence is presented to the Grand Jury, and what witness testimony is heard.

Prosecutors work with police every day on a variety of cases and depend on police for investigations as well as witness testimony to get convictions. Without the police the prosecutor's case doesn't exist. Without the prosecutor the police can't get the bad guys off the street. Police and Prosecutors must work closely together as one unit to up hold and administer the laws in name of the people. The relationship between police and prosecutors give reason to believe there is a secret subculture in law enforcement.

When police officers commit crimes to whose best interest does the prosecutors work, the citizens, the police, a political agenda, or their own. Regardless of how it may seem it appears to be a great big conflict of interest, and the people lose. It is highly known policemen face difficult decision every people have come to expect policeman to be protectors, social workers, referees, and emergency first responders. People expect police officers to give unconditional "loyalty to their community versus loyalty to their fellow officers." Police departments across the country have officers swear an oath to "serve and protect without allowing "personal feelings, prejudices, animosities, or friendships" influencing their character, attitudes or behavior." In every city in America police officer's work alongside each other on the streets, and also in some of the worst environments, under the most dangerous conditions.

Most too often policeman's "cop code" develops in where secrets are kept, and officers "often hide information and maintain a code of silence to protect fellow officers." Conflicting agendas have social consequences within communities because officers do not play by the rules. Secret subcultures "foster a sense of distrust and disrespect of the police department." African American and "minority neighborhoods," People now regard the police as a threat and also a front for racial discrimination. Because of the change in the perception people have of police become less cooperative and less willing to communicate with police assisting in reporting and solving crimes.

A good example of extreme cases is the high number of police shootings of unarmed citizens. Police secrets and injustice create act of civil disobedience, and also civil unrest might also occur. According to Lawrence, N., ["law enforcement code of ethics is composed of three parts. The first part concerns equal protection. Police officers must enforce the law regardless of the race, sex, class, or identity of the offender. Secondly, police must follow the law themselves. Civil liberties cannot be violated. Thirdly, they are held to a moral standard above and beyond that of many members of the public. They are not allowed to use their power for personal gain or live immorally."

In addition Lawrence stated ["some cops develop a personal code of ethics in which loyalty to their fellow officers trumps serving and protecting the community. This tribal mentality can be attributed to three causes. First of all, police officers are an identifiable group with uniforms, badges and guns. Secondly, this group shares a common way of life. They share similar dangers, setbacks, and rewards that outsiders rarely see outside of the movies. Thirdly, these dangers foster an "us against them" mentality not just against criminals but politicians, bureaucrats and concerned citizens who are perceived as impediments to enforcing the law."] Regardless of the secrets hidden within law enforcement, society has no other choice but depend on law enforcement to expose the harmful and deadly secrets of those who pose a threat to the safety and security of the people. More transparency would help expose secrets within law enforcement.

Chapter Seven

Ordinary People

But what about the human factor? More transparency would help expose secrets within law enforcement, but what about the human factor? Police officers are people too and have personal secrets unknown to even the agencies and departments they work. It appears everyone has a secret; fact is they would not be secrets if others knew the things you or others may keep to yourself. We never know what others may be hiding or thinking at any given time. Yet we go through each day in direct contact with people trusting them on faith or how they react under the conditions we see them. However if someone was hiding a secret do you think they would let anyone know it?

People start their lives each under the assumption nothing will happen that will disrupt their day. Most people focus only on themselves and what they are trying to achieve and not what is going on around them involving others. Many times people ignore information or warnings of things that are happening or about to happen. People go to bed with only how their day ended and how they expect the next day to begin thinking of no one or nothing but themselves. Waking up the next morning while they are dressing they listen to the radio or watch TV, bad news through the media is all they hear or see. While some have breakfast and read a paper as their feet hit the floor receive more bad news before they walk out the door.

Many people try to solve their problems after school or work, road rage have others acting like jerks. This may be the very day a random shooting occur at the place they believe to be their safe haven. The whole world has problems this people should see, and start thinking of others instead of individually. It is always the unexpected or the unknown that hurts us the most. People of our society place the entire burden of safety and securities in the hands of government to protect the citizens from secret attacks or life altering events. The people hold the government accountable for the actions of ordinary people with hidden secrets. However this also turns the other the other way the government knew of the plans of the 911 attacks. Even with information the government has from more than 17 intelligence agencies no information has been given to the public about how much the government knew and how they knew it.

Over the years government demands and gets the trust and confidence of the people, but do not willing to give that same trust and confidence. For more than sixty years the government still has disclosed what was found in Roswell New Mexico, or the real reason for area fifty one. After more than fifty years the government still keeps much of the Kennedy assignation classified and top secret. Does anyone know what happened to Teamsters President and Boss Jimmy Hoffa? Many readers may not remember those people or events because they were not born, yet it is part of our history hidden in time.

Some politicians, government officials and Presidential Administrations have always view and treated the general population of America as adolescent children that cannot understand or tolerate the truth. Most people focus on the reasons or lies politicians tell to the public to satisfy their concerns. Very few people question the reasons for the information easily given. Many times information is given to give the perception of transparency to cover other secret actions carried out by the government. Everyone now knows there were no weapons of mass destruction in Iraq, the invasion and war was about regime change. However the bigger secret is that was an action kept secret looking for an excuse since the early 1970s and the exile of the Shaw of Iran and emergence of the Ayatollah.

The United States always wanted to make their presence known in the Middle East in the oil producing countries. Even now in 2018 the top leaders in government keep secrets not only from congress but the entire country. Only one man in America knows what agreement was mad with America's Russian adversary during a private meeting droning a summit between the countries. Other secrets that have a direct effect on your family's safety, security and future is what was said and what agreements were made at the summit in Singapore between the North Korean Leadership and the President of the United States. The American people have the right to know what secrets are over shadowing their lives.

There are more than 3000 lies and just as many secrets seeping from there hiding places from the investigation by a special prosecutor exposing the facts and truth. The secrets of more than six people have been exposed and six people have pleaded guilty of crimes. The guilty pleas from those six is in addition to at least thirteen indictments of individuals who secretly collaborated in collusion and conspiracy in attacking the United States elections. In lite of how serious as these allegations are and the harm they did to the country, the people must not focus on one man's secrets. One man or one small group can solve all of America's problems. Many of the things that are tearing down and destroying people's lives in America begins closer to their homes, in their neighborhoods and communities. Anything that is done that includes the public or members of society is not private and should not be kept as a secret from society.

Living as part of society people must become more vigilant of their environmental surroundings and the people that make up their community. People must stop being instantly acceptable to word they hear, every idea expressed, and each offer made without questioning motive or verifying with supporting evidence and facts. People must stop being enablers allowing wrong or bad things to exist in their communities and accepting the consequences without taking responsibility for not speaking out against them. People know of drug dealers in their communities and keep their secret from police until they make addicts of their child.

People know of those addicted to drugs yet keep it to themselves until they break into their home or rob them on the street. People know of the thirty year old man that befriend teenage girls and say nothing until one become missing or turn up dead. People know police officers who will look the other way for sexual favors or cash. People know police officers who will pull traffic tickets or have their friends that are officers tear them up. Police officers who are dating your friend or your daughter but stand by and say nothing when other officers are brutalizing or shooting your son are in every department. These are just some of the secrets that are hiding in every community in the country. By not exposing these secrets people are enablers contributing to their own sorrows or doom. In 20013 ["police went to the home of Ariel Castro on at least one occasion at the time he was holding three young ladies captive for almost ten years.

One of the women, 27-year old Amanda Berry, managed to escape and phone 911 that officers came and got them to freedom. With Ariel Castro, 52, and brothers Pedro, 54, and Oil Castro, 50, in custody and awaiting charges, authorities have come under scrutiny for how they missed clues that Berry and two other young women were being kept as prisoners in the rundown home in the city's west side neighborhood. Berry, whom police called a hero for breaking out of the house Monday and summoning help, had disappeared in 2003 when she was 16. Michelle Knight went missing in 2002, when she was 20. Gina DeJesus, then 14, was reported missing in 2004."]

It is hard to believe no one in the neighborhood noticed anything different in Castro's behavior or demeanor over a ten year period. No one in the neighborhood tried to befriend him a hold conversation. If his secret was not exposed how many more young ladies would he have held captive? In Tuttle, Oklahoma 23 year old Gregory Zavala ["was accused of raping and assaulting three teenage girls. Zavala was accused of holding them captive at his remote Tuttle, Oklahoma, home for months at a time and faces three counts of kidnapping, two counts of child sexual abuse, two counts of assault and battery with a dangerous weapon and rape. Zavala allegedly enticed the three women at different times and got two of them pregnant between 2011 and 2013 at the home he shared with his parents.

Zavala allegedly threatened to kill each victim and their families if they ever left his house, according to an affidavit filed with police."] In over three years not even his parents stumbled into Zavala secrets. Zavala's mother and father living in the same house never knew who was coming or going or who the person living in their house really was. Sometimes parents have secrets that involve illicit acts with their own children. In Pennsylvania Mr. and Mrs. Daniel and Savilla Stoltzfus both in their early forties was an Amish couple "who told police they gifted their 14-year-old daughter to a man who helped save their farm have were arrested along with the man."

Daniel Stoltzfus and his wife Savilla Stoltzfus gave their daughter, who is not being named, to 51-year-old Feasterville man Lee Kaplan in 2012, and the couple apparently moved in with him. All three were arrested after child welfare workers discovered Kaplan's home housed 11 other girls aged between six month and 18 years, two of whom he had fathered with the couple's daughter. Police were called to Kaplan's after a neighbor complained about child abuse in the house. Entering the house police officers found Kaplan and all 12 girls. The couple was apparently living there also according to police. However, it's not known how long they had been living there, why they moved in or what had happened to their own home. The Stoltzfuses told police they were going to lose their farm until Kaplan 'came out of the blue and saved them from financial ruin' around four years ago, said Bucks County District Attorney."]

["In return, the couple gave Kaplan their daughter, who was then 14. Daniel Stoltzfus said that he thought the transaction was legal after researching online. Kaplan impregnated the 14-year-old almost immediately after she entered his home, and again when she was 17 years-old. The girl is now 18, police said, and her three-year-old and six-month-old children were living in Kaplan's house. According to the criminal complaint, Savilla Stoltzfus was aware that Kaplan was having sex with her daughter."] One child was raped at age fourteen and eleven other children being abused, but the secrets stayed locked in a Darkhouse. Sometimes it pays to have curious neighbors.

But it is not always old dark houses on dead end streets that hold the secrets or the stranger in town that acts differently than the people around you all the time. Sometimes the evil destructive secrets are kept by someone well known and well respected. The television news show 60 Minutes aired a segment about a well-known doctor with outstanding professional practice, and also what most people believed to be high integrity who had deep dark secrets. 60 Minutes aired the story of Lawrence Nassar considered a world-renowned sports physician treating America's foremost Olympic women gymnasts. Nassar was arrested and charged after ["three former members of the U.S. National Gymnastics team, one of them an Olympic medalist, describe for the first time the sexual abuse they say they were subjected to at the hands of the team's doctor, Lawrence Nassar. The women's attorney, who has filed a law suit against USA Gymnastics for failing to protect the women, believes there were more than a hundred athletes that may have been abused dating back to the 1996 Olympic Games."]

Dr. Nassar at this time is being held on charges of criminal sexual conduct and possession of child pornography unrelated to the Gymnastics team, convinced women and girls that he was performing medical treatment they required."] One of the women ["Jessica Howard was the U.S. National champion in rhythmic gymnastics from 1999 to 2001. She recalls one session with Dr. Nassar and stated "He started massaging me and had asked me not to wear any underwear.

And then he just continued to go into more and more intimate places." Also saying "I remember thinking something was off but I didn't feel like I was able to say anything because he was, you know, this very high profile doctor," says Howard. The girls questioned Nassar's behavior among themselves. "The girls would say 'yeah he touches you funny,'" she recalls. Jeanette Antolin, who competed with the U.S. National Team from 1995 to 2000, felt that way, too."] Jeanette Antolin stated ["I remember being uncomfortable because of the area. But in my mind, I was like, 'If this helps, I'll do anything.'" Still trying to maintain trust in the doctor she did not complain believing at the time "It was treatment, and you don't complain about treatment."] The story goes on telling "California attorney John Manly represents Howard, Antolin and more than 40 others, including a woman who was 9 years old when the alleged abuse took place."

["He says Nassar abused many more women. "We know that at least 60 have come forward, but my best estimate is it's in the hundreds and possibly more," he tells LaPook. Manly believes the alleged abuse began over 20 years ago. "I believe that at the end of the day, there are members of every single Olympic team since 1996 he did this."] During the broad cast it was reported ["USA Gymnastics declined to speak with 60 Minutes on camera. In written statements, the organization said those five weeks after it learned of a complaint about Dr. Nassar in 2015; it relieved Nassar of his duties with the national team and notified the FBI."]

Chapter Eight

Protecting Secrets

Doctors are human and think act and deceive like ordinary people. This make everyone understand why years ago ethical and moral regulations were established forbidding male doctors to examine or treating female patients without a nurse present; it appears doctor, Lawrence Nassar made himself the exception to the rule and fund a way around it. By now readers may be thinking of ways to expose secrets to protect themselves. However before you can expose a secret you first must know how to protect a secret. Neither governments nor people can protect themselves from a secret; reason being you cannot protect yourself from something you do not know, that is the purpose and function of a secret to be unknown.

Secrets are protected by lies and discerption, a false cover that shine like gold to blind you to the truth and facts of harmful or deadly behavior. People with corrupt intent go through extreme measures to protect their secrets. Protecting secrets people become proficient pathological liars as the first line of defense. Lying about a secret gives someone plausible deniability to the acts in question or the secrets exposed. The bigger the lie the more it is accepted and the harder it is to find the truth, and the longer a secret can hide and the safer it is. If a secret become known to one other person or a very small group of people, the person with the secret may try paying them to keep in secret. In many situations people are threaten with exposing harmful or embarrassing information they may have, threaten their families, threaten them with violence or death, or in some cases kill them or have them killed.

Serial killers and murders kill their witnesses and anyone who can expose their secret. Unfortunately serial killers and murders are not the only ones that will kill to protect their secrets. Kidnappers, serial rapist, and child molesters will also kill to maintain a secret and avoid exposure. Drug dealers and street gangs have been known to use violence and murder to keep secrets to avoid exposure, capture and incarceration. Using threat of violence or death to protect a secret is how the term was phrased (snitches get stiches) used on the streets. The most common practice of protecting secrets is the three D's distraction, diversion, and division.

Distractions cause people to lose focus on the issues at hand by creating a false narrative. Diversions cause people to look for answers in another direction other than where the secrets are hiding by changing the narrative to fit the distraction. Distractions and diversions cause a division among the people causing people to be undecided on who or what to believe. No one uses distraction, diversion, and division to hide secrets better than the wealthy, politicians, or the government. The wealthy use money to create situations to manipulate media allowing them to see everything they do to make news to distract from the original subject, make big business deals, make new large purchases, or sale of assets, announce weddings or separations of businesses or in relationships whatever attracts media attention. Doctors, Lawyers, and Politicians protect secrets by creating Diversions with false narratives and using loopholes in the laws.

Doctors, Lawyers, and Politicians use methods and tactics as classified, confidentially, and executive privilege to hide their secrets. The government hides the secrets in plain sight labeled "TOP SECRET" National Security file it away in the national archives for more than fifty years. According to the "Information Security Oversight Office," ["Government policies dictate that any piece of classified information is "owned" by the Executive agency which created it, even if the record itself is no longer (or never was) in the custody of that agency. Agencies determine the ongoing sensitivity of their information, or "equity," and mandate its protection accordingly.

Declassification is a determination that information would no longer damage national security if released, and no longer warrants withholding from the public."] Laws and corruption protect secrets for the privileged, but what of the rest of society. Many people may find this hard to believe but remember it has been more than fifty years and all the information and facts about the John F. Kennedy assignation have not been released to the public. Right now many of you are wondering how the regular citizen or common person hides their secrets. Every day citizens use the three the D's but at a different level with a slightly different outcome. Everyone has confidentiality rights by law with their attorney and religious councilor or priest. But also many middle class, low income and poor people don't have personal attorneys, and also many more stopped attending church or want to hear from clergy: keeping secrets from them also.

Diversions with by creating false narratives are the main method of protecting secrets in the general population. Lying and persuading or influencing others to lie is typical of people without financial support or resources to create deniability and cover-ups. Secrets within the general population almost never reach the national security level or effect people outside of their communities. Secrets within the general population commonly revolve around problems or issues as who is embezzling money from the employer or stealing from their job, who's robbing the local businesses or burglarizing homes in neighborhood the community.

Other secrets involving crime refers to who committed the drive by shooting, where drugs are bought and sold and who's responsible. These types of secrets are usually protected by influencing family or friends to provide the cover of silence through rewarding them with small incentives as cash or favors making them accomplices, accessories, or enablers of the secret. In some cases those secrets are kept through the use of fear of retaliation or street law (snitches wear stiches) or violent threats against families or friends. However rich or poor no secret is ever safe because they all have one thing in common, no one is willing to sacrifice their life to go to prison or die for someone's secret. In spite of all the life altering or life or death secrets it appears the number one secret that asserts itself in all circles of life concerns relationships. From neighborhood gossip circles, beauty shop, barber shop, and tabloids to the national media everyone wants to know who's sleeping with whom?

When it comes to protecting relationship secrets people appear to have no ethics or morals. Protecting relationship secrets people appear to have no shame, respect or conscious of guilt using their mothers and family, friends and employers to hide their secrets. People will get their love ones to lie, pretend to work over-time on their job, and claim to have business meetings, out of town conferences, week end excursions with or for their boss, or family emergencies out of town. These protections only work when people don't include their spouse or companion involvement in their life away from home.

Chapter Nine

Technology and secrets

Many times long distance truck drivers and military personnel use their jobs and technology to hide secretes there are many individuals with corrupt or ill moral intent attempt to use modern technology in their dirty deeds. Many people that occupation takes them away from home for extended periods of time lead double lives. However some of them find innovative ways to cheat on their spouses with convincing evidence through technology. To keep track of their spouse they will call home to keep their spouse in place. When they are at home these calls allow them to know where their spouse is at all times to prevent running into them by accident. Some people use GPS tracking on their phones and their spouse's phone so each one can know where the other is. When out of town after making the call home for the night leave their phone in the hotel room and pretend to have it on vibrate while you sleep. Their spouses GPS will show them to be in their room while they are out on the town.

Military personnel cannot carry electronic communications devices on active duty they can never be tracked, electronic devices give away their location to the enemy. There are also many people secretly using two cell phones, one for home and one for outside activity. But cell phones create one problem too much information can be stored inside that can be retrieved. Many secrets are taken from cell phones such as text messages and social media communications.

People try to hide their secrets and claim to want to keep things private and confidential, yet store all their secrets and personal information in cell phones or on computers. No secrets are safe floating around in cyber space: Private Citizens are just more venerable if not more than businesses and incorporations. Inter Net providers and social media sites collect your information and create profiles detailing your habits, lifestyle, financial institutions, shopping and travel habits. The main thing profiled on everyone is their shopping habits by ethnicity, race, age group and environment you live for target marking. In addition the information is sold to other company's over and over again. People give away their secrets and there is no privacy in the cyber world, the only secrets are people don't know their lives were being invaded. The governments of some country's support cyber-attacks and hacking America.

According to Kharpal, A.["Chinese state-backed hackers have carried out a string of cyber espionage attacks on U.S. companies, violating a pact signed by the two countries to stop carrying out this kind of activity, according to a cybersecurity company. The U.S. technology and pharmaceutical sectors have been subject to attacks aimed at the "theft of intellectual property and trade secrets" in the last three weeks, according to U.S group CrowdStrike, which says it has blocked all of the attempted intrusions."] Along with stealing business, financial and technological private information of private citizens was also taken.

"The United States and China signed an agreement in which the world's two largest economies agreed not to steal corporate data for economic benefit." ["Seven of the companies are firms in the technology or pharmaceuticals sectors, where the intrusions aligned to facilitate theft of intellectual property and trade secrets, rather than conducting national-security related intelligence collection the Cyber agreement does not prohibit."] ["Cybercrime is an increasingly specific concern for American citizens and organizations, according to one finance expert that pointed out as many as one billion data records were hacked and stolen in the US alone. The study that provided this information asserted theft of credit card data is the number one concern for Americans, followed by having a smartphone or computer attacked and information accessed.

"There are 80 to 90 million plus cybersecurity events per year, with close to 400 new threats every minute, and up to 70 percent of attacks going undetected,"] The United States Government is playing catch-up in the cyber war that has been in attack on the country and the citizens for quite some time. This is another one of the secrets the government was keeping until it was leaked to the media who exposed it to the public. If the government and Silicon Valley are playing catch-up, and now working together to address these issues, what must the citizens protect their information? There is a giant difference between Privacy and Secrets; one must understand privacy is a joyous activity or event involving one and their family or companion.

However, someone's desire for privacy is known to everyone. Privacy has no connection to the neighborhood, community, or society. Privacy is a personal state without intrusion from others or intruding on others. Whereas secrets are harmful, dangerous, and catastrophic to everyone involved in something people want unknown. Secrets always cause conflict, anger, and deceit and only exposed over time. Someone always takes a loss or lose their life because of secrets. If secrets were not evil why do people keep them hidden? Although now it appears all information must hidden to the point that it would be hard to determine was true or false, personal or public.

CBS News reported ["crime is a very real threat in our Internet-connected society. With 1.5 million annual cyber-attacks, online crime is a real threat to anyone on the Internet. That number means there are over 4,000 cyber-attacks every day, 170 attacks every hour, or nearly three attacks every minute. When you look at number of attacks specifically targeting businesses, they're also worrying: IBM estimates businesses are attacked an average of 16,856 times a year. That's 46 attacks every business has to deal with every day or nearly two attacks an hour. Though the vast majority of these attacks don't actually get past a corporation's defenses, an average of 1.7 per week is that adds up across all businesses, which is too many successful cyber-attacks."] Should the general public worried about cyber-attacks when most hackers and cyber criminals target businesses and governments?

The answer is a definitely yes: because huge organizations hold caches of individual information that become useful for identity theft and other crimes and make tempting targets for cyber criminals. Although you have no control over organizations protect or use information once they gain access to it, it only makes good sense to be aware of whom you share your personal or private information. A cyber-attack by Chinese hackers, resulting in the theft of hospital patients Social Security numbers and other personal data belonging to 4.5 million people. The attackers appear to be a sophisticated hacking group that has hacked into major U.S. companies throughout several industries, according to The FBI is reportedly investigating the case. Citizens "Social Security numbers and other personal data are stolen by cybercriminals to sell on underground black markets for use by others in identity theft" schemes.

However the Chinese are not the only foreign country launching cyberattacks against American citizens, businesses, and the United States Government. Cyber-attacks from Russia resembled a full scale cyber war. Russia secretly enacted a cyber invasion on the United States as early as 2013. The Russian cyber-attack was not widely publicize by the government or the media in the name of national security while an extensive investigation was being conducted and counter measures were asserted to safeguard the infrastructure that had already been hacked into. Homeland Security and the FBI were unaware of the extent of the cyberattack.

Russian hackers lay dormant to go undetected until they can launch their real objective. By now they had already stolen personal information of American citizens, and begin recruiting help from Americans. Over the next two years the Russian worked at establishing false identities as Americans online. However during the Russian invasion in 2013 an American businessman and celebrity traveled to Russia to produce and direct a beauty pageant. One year earlier this businessman had publicly expressed in intentions at pursuing further interest at running for president. While in Russia he continued the behavior he was custom at home and allegedly committed acts that were compromising him with the Russian government. In addition he was pursuing business interest in building a hotel in Russia.

There is nothing illegal or wrong with Americans doing business in other countries, but there was something that occurred causing this venture to become a secret. For more than two years nothing more was said about Russia or their activities. Believing enough time had passed by since his trip to Russia, the business took advantage of an opportunity of a country in search of new leadership entered the run for the presidency. While "Neil Young's "Rockin' In The Free World" played in the lobby of Trump Tower on Fifth Avenue in New York City." Carrying a closet full of secrets "the real estate and reality television mogul descended an escalator to his own presidential announcement."

Chapter Ten

Sorting Secrets

The businessman thought he had the only key to the closet where he kept his skeletons, but that prove to be wrong, running for public office especially president of the United States life becomes an open book. However there were so many secrets it was almost impossible to sort them all out. The more digging around and searching the closet, the more important and damaging the secrets would get. The first skeleton in the closet was his tax returns that were cast to the side because of his insisting he was under audit, but the truth is there were things more damaging the public needed to know.

Other secrets that would usually disqualify any other presidential begun to surface but only a minor effect on his ratings: his opponent's popularity was not much higher than his.

Even though the further into the dark closet of skeletons investigators and media went the more discrediting secrets would be exposed to the light of truth. Secrets were exposed that pierced the hearts of many Americans which there were no excuses. Three divorces that would many times mean nothing became secrets after it was alleged he had raped one of his wives. However what made it scandals is all three former wives were forced to sign none disclosure Agreements (NDA'S) and paid large amounts of cash. Also secrets of alleged spousal abuse, numerous illicit affairs with porn stars and models, and girls in his beauty pageants. There were secrets of fraud, a history of family corruption that would take months to investigate. There were secrets of allegations of sexual misconduct that he admitted while on a bus tour, but later denied, and also paid hundreds of thousands of dollars to cover-up and keep quite.

There was also many other illicit business secrets no one would expect from a self-proclaimed billionaire worth tens of billions of dollars. The businessman candidate found himself falling way behind his opponent in the race. To regain the lead in the ratings he asserted the three D's (Distraction, diversion, and division), but also this move put him at risk of exposing more corruption and illicit secrets. Running a smear campaign was not working to his satisfaction when he during a rally on national television ask Russia to intervene in the U.S. national election.

His words and actions were perfectly clear, the world heard him say "Russia if your listening I hope you can find the 30,000 emails that are missing, I believe you will be rewarded mightily by the press." The very same night within hours Russian hackers began their attacks on the democratic National Committee's computer system. His plea to Russia ignited an investigation that would lead into many other dark secrets kept in his closet. WiKi Leaks Started dropping stolen emails on the internet as he went hard and steady with his smear tactics and propaganda. Misleading information leaked to the FBI cause them to reopen the investigation into his opponent's missing emails. For some unfortunate reason the director of the FBI released that information to the media and ended any chance for his opponent to win. The candidate is now the President of the United States; however the Special Prosecutor's investigation into Russian hacking and interference in the 2016 elections is ongoing.

The special investigation has exposed many secrets of the president's election campaign. The special investigation exposed secrets of collusion of six top staff members of the president's campaign and even more Russian who were involved. According to Prokop, A. ["either indictments or guilty pleas from 19 people and three companies that we know of were exposed by special council Mueller's team has. That group is composed of four former advisers, 13 Russian nationals, three Russian companies, one California man, and one London-based lawyer."]

Also "Five of these people (including three former aides) have already pleaded guilty." However,[" None of the charges against Americans or his advisers so far have directly alleged that they worked with Russia to interfere with the campaign. Michael Flynn and George Papadopoulos have pleaded guilty to making false statements about their contacts with Russians to investigators. Paul Manafort and Rick Gates were hit with tax, money laundering and other charges that relate to their work for the government of Ukraine and a Russia-affiliated Ukrainian political party. In all the evidence gathered everything is beginning to connect to the White House."] Taking into consideration the relationship of the people charged there is little doubt the president was tied to the corruption. ["George Papadopoulos, campaign foreign policy adviser, pleaded guilty in October to making false statements to the FBI. Michael Flynn, the President's national security adviser, pleaded guilty in December to making false statements to the FBI.

Paul Manafort, the President's campaign chair, was indicted in October in Washington, DC on charges of conspiracy, money laundering, and false statements, all related to Ukrainian politicians before he joined the campaign. He's pleaded not guilty on all counts. Then, in February, Mueller filed a new case against him in Virginia, with tax, financial, and bank fraud charges. Rick Gates, a former campaign aide and Manafort's longtime junior business partner, was indicted on similar charges to Manafort.

But in February he agreed to a plea deal with Mueller's team, pleading guilty to just one false statements charge and one conspiracy charge. 13 Russian nationals and three Russian companies were indicted on conspiracy charges, with some also being accused of identity theft The charges related to a Russian propaganda effort designed to interfere with the 2016 campaign."] "The companies involved are the Internet Research Agency, often described as a "Russian troll farm," and two other companies that helped finance it." ["The Russian nationals indicted include 12 of the agency's employees and its alleged financier, Yevgeny Prigozhin. Richard Pinedo: This California man pleaded guilty to an identity theft charge in connection with the Russian indictments, and has agreed to cooperate with Mueller."]

"Alex van der Zwaan: This London lawyer pleaded guilty to making false statements to the FBI about his contacts with Rick Gates and another unnamed person based in Ukraine." Only an insane person would believe corruption is the best way to exonerate people with criminal intent from crimes they have committed."] The president continues to lie and deny any involvement with Russia, but the facts show differently. No one knows how this will end as the investigations are ongoing and secrets are still being exposed. The closet door is open and the skeletons have come to life, but also time is running out. The reckless actions of the president only prove what his secrets have reviled; he is leading the country to destruction.

Secrets do not build they destroy and lying hide secrets. How can America move forward when every word from the president's mouth is a lie covering another secret? However it will not be the actions of one man that destroy America. It will not be an act of nature or nuclear war that brings the country to the brink of destruction, it will be the secrets. America is on the path of desolation behind the millions of secrets ill morality people hold in the neighborhoods and communities. But also America is a victim of the secrets of unethical behavior of the business, secrets of rape, murder, robbery and theft of criminals, and secrets of corruption of politicians and law enforcement. It is not the general population and majority of the people that destroy America, nor will it be foreign bombs or nuclear explosions. Nature will find a way to adjust and climate change will balance itself. The desolation of America will come from too many secrets hiding the evil behind catastrophic greed, dishonest politicians, an unmanaged military and the financial complex that fund and support it.

Nor will our society end because of Christian extremist and racial supremacist, deliberate disinformation and propaganda, an uneducated population of followers with no leadership, and voter apathy and suppression that fosters Authoritarians with personality disorders. The death to America will come from too many evil secrets, but time will expose them all.

Acknowledgements

Abbasi, W. USA TODAY Jason Stockley verdict shows how rare
	officer convictions are in police shootings retrieved from
	https://www.usatoday.com/story/news/nation/2017/06/17/convi

Allen, B. Book documents molestation in conservative Baptist
	churches January 27, 2016 retrieved from
	https://baptistnews.com/article/book-documents-molestation-
	in-conservative-baptist-churches/#.W7fdv_ZFy00

Articles of Impeachment retrieved from
	http://watergate.info/impeachment/articles-of-impeachment

Associated Press, Former Mississippi teacher charged with sex crimes,
	retrieved from
	https://www.hattiesburgamerican.com/story/news/crime/2014/0
	8/21/former-mississippi-teacher-charged-with-sex-crime

Bachrach, J. What's Behind Donald Trump's Obsession with Beauty
	Pageants? Photo retrieved from
	https://www.vanityfair.com/news/2016/01/donald-trump-miss-
	universe-beauty-pageants

BBC News, Reagan and the 'Iran-Contra' affair retrieved from
	http://news.bbc.co.uk/2/hi/americas/269619.stm

Berlinger, J. and Smith-Spark, L. CNN Top adviser to Pope charged
	with sexual assault offenses retrieved from
	https://www.cnn.com/2017/06/28/asia/cardinal-pell-
	australia/index.html

Acknowledgements

Bundy, Ted Biography Author Biography.com Editors Website Name the Biography.com retrieved from https://www.biography.com/people/ted-bundy-9231165 October 2, 2018 A&E Television Networks Last Updated July 16, 2018 Original Published Date April 2, 2014

Catholic Church photos retrieved from https://www.bing.com/images/search?view=detailV2&ccid=JTzVQG3Y&id=A61FF692242CC8C017A502CFD18623AF48DD713F&thid=OIP.JTzVQG3Yzwm2LiF4Vub0

CBS News These Cybercrime Statistics Will Make You Think Twice About Your Password: Where's the CSI Cyber team when you need them? Retrieved from https://www.cbs.com/shows/csi-cyber/news/1003888/these-cybercrime-statistics-will-make-you-think-twice-about-your-password-where-s-the-csi-cyber-team-when-you-need-th

CBS News, 60 Minutes, Team USA doctor allegedly masked sexual abuse as treatments, retrieved from https://www.cbsnews.com/news/team-usa-doctor-allegedly-disguised-sexual-abuse-as-treatments/

Dahmer, J. Biography, Biography.com Editors, the Biography.com website retrieved from https://www.biography.com/people/jeffrey-dahmer-9264755

Acknowledgements

October 2, 2018 A&E Television Networks August 1, 2017 Original
     Published Date April 2, 2014

"Du Bois W.E.B., THE SOULS OF BLACK FOLK," retrieved from
     http://www.wwnorton.com/college/history/give-me-
     liberty4/docs/WEBDuBois-Souls_of_Black_Folk-1903.pdf

Falcone, M. Donald Trump Rode an Escalator to 2016 Presidential
     Announcement retrieved from
     https://abcnews.go.com/Politics/donald-trump-rode-escalator-
     2016-presidential-announcement/story?id=31801433

George Bush 43 photo retrieved from
     https://www.bing.com/images/search?view=detailV2&ccid=8P
     UQz0G3&id=0CD1745D34352B6934B34F206BBDDD882B6
     448B1&thid=OIP.8PUQz0G37

Grim, R., Sledge, M. and Ferner, M., Key Figures in CIA-Crack
     Cocaine Scandal Begin to Come Forward retrieved from
     https://www.huffingtonpost.com/2014/10/10/gary-webb-dark-
     alliance_n_5961748.html

Griffin, Al, Two Men Convicted of Child Sex Crimes in Camden
     County Are Sentenced retrieved from
     https://www.lakeexpo.com/news/crime/two-men-convicted-of-
     child-sex-crimes-in-camden-county/article_af7e0260-47fc-
     11e8-8949-2b757b1d2ead.html

Acknowledgements

Harvey Weinstein Photo retrieved from opixusac.tpanel.nl/harvey-weinstein-facebook.php?i=1

Hill, C. Baptist pastor and principal arrested for sex crimes in Rockingham County retrieved from spectrumlocalnews.com/nc/charlotte/news/2018/08/31/baptist-pastor-and-principal-arrested-for-sex-crimes-in-rockingham-county-victory-baptist-church-kevin-scott-heffner

Information Security Oversight Office, Identifying and handling Classified Records in Private Papers retrieved from https://www.archives.gov/isoo/faqs/identifying-handling-classified-records.html

Jenkins, J. P. John Wayne Gacy article retrieved from https://www.britannica.com/biography/John-Wayne-Gacy

John Wayne Gacy, photo retrieved from https://www.bing.com/images/search?q=John+Wayne+Gacy&FORM=IDINTS

Kavanagh, Brett retrieved from https://www.bing.com/images/search?q=pictures+of+kavanagh+in+hearing&id=52EDEF6491CE49DACB69E21EA4A1B89E48A54615&FORM=IQFRBA

Kharpal, A, is China still hacking US? This cyber firm says yes article retrieved from https://www.cnbc.com/2015/10/19/china-hacking-us-companies-for-secrets-despite-cyber-pact-.html

Acknowledgements

Lawrence, N. Police Subcultures vs. Law Enforcement Code of Ethics, retrieved from https://legalbeagle.com/6320027-police-law-enforcement-code-ethics.html

"LawFirms" "Teacher Sex Offender List: 25 Female Teacher and Student Sex Crime Scandals." Retrieved from www.lawfirms.com/female-teacher-sex-crime-offenders-and-sc

Lyndon B. Johnson photo retrieved from www.sickchirpse.com/wp-content/uploads/2017/10/Lyndon-B.-Johnson--1000x579.jpg

Mccormack, D. Captor 'lured three teenage girls into his parents' house, held them prisoner for months and got two of them pregnant' article retrieved from https://www.dailymail.co.uk/news/article-3012906/Captor-lured-three-teenage-girls-parents-house-held-prisoner-months-got-two-pregnant.htm

Miltimore, J. Why Are So Many Female Teachers Sleeping With Students? Retrieved from https://www.intellectualtakeout.org/blog/why-are-so-many-female-teachers-sleeping-students

Mystal, E., "Judge Roy Moore Allegedly Had Sexual Encounter with Underage Girl When He" Was a District Attorney, retrieved from https://abovethelaw.com/2017/11/judge-roy-moore-allegedly-had-sexual-encounter-with-underage-girl-when-he-was-a-district-attorney/

Acknowledgements

Novus ordo Seclorum (n.d.) Dictionary.com Unabridged Retrieved

Oliver North Biography, retrieved from

https://www.biography.com/people/oliver-north-9425102

Park, M. Timeline: A look at the Catholic Church's sex abuse scandals article retrieved from

https://www.cnn.com/2017/06/29/world/timeline-catholic-church-sexual-abuse-scandals/index.html

Pease, J. freelance writer, ex- evangelical pastor, the sin of silence retrieved from

https://www.washingtonpost.com/news/posteverything/wp/2018/05/31/feature/the-epidemic-of-denial-about-sexual-abuse-in-t

Prokop, A., All of Robert Mueller's indictments and plea deals in the Russia investigation so far article retrieved from

https://www.vox.com/policy-and-politics/2018/2/20/17031772/mueller-indictments-grand-jury

Psychology One, Personality disorders retrieved from

http://www.psychone.net/list-of-personality-disorders.php

Richard Nixon photo retrieved from http://www.history.com/topics/us-presidents/richard-m-nixon/pictures/richard-nixon/richard-nixon-raising-his-arms-to-crowd

Ronald Reagan photo retrieved from

https://www.bing.com/images/search?view=detailV2&ccid=qa

wd6f6H&id=0E10BE442DAC894ACB2BB384B351F0F7B3B

Acknowledgements

Royals, C. Why Lie? Retrieved from

https://www.amazon.com/dp/1976811112/ref=sr_1_1?s=digital

text&ie=UTF8&qid=1515171540&sr=81&keywords=Why+Li

e%3F%3A+2018+Midterm+Culture+War+By+Charles+Royal

Royals, C. Lunatic / Criminal Asylum at 1600 retrieved from Amazon

Books

https://www.amazon.com/dp/1981030379?ref_=pe_870760_15

REUTERS and SZATHMARY, Z. Personal data belonging to

4.5MILLION American hospital patients stolen in cyber-attack

by Chinese article retrieved from

https://www.dailymail.co.uk/news/article-2728347/Personal-

data-belonging-4-5MILLION-Americans-stolen-cyber-attack-

Chinese.html

SCHINDLER, P., Trump Loses, but Roy Moore Is the Booby Prize

Photo retrieved from

https://www.gaycitynews.nyc/stories/2017/20/w28519-trump-

loses-roy-moore-booby-prize-2017-09-28.html

Stacklin, J. Authorities visited home of Cleveland man accused of

holding 3 women captive article retrieved from

https://www.yahoo.com/news/blogs/lookout/escaped-

cleveland-woman-amanda-berry-real-hero-kidnapping-14144

Skeleton in closet, Photographer: Johner Images retrieved from

https://l7.alamy.com/zooms/46fb51967da54214bb3c10fed5d27

Acknowledgements

Ted Bundy, photo retrieved from

     https://www.pinterest.com/explore/ted-bundy/

Thomas, K. cybersecurity: 70% attack goes unchecked article retrieved

     from https://www.welivesecurity.com/2015/09/09/cybercrime-

Trueman, C. N. "Lyndon Johnson and Vietnam" Retrieved from

     http://www.historylearningsite.co.uk/vietnam-war/lyndon-joh

True Crime Daily, Ex-church daycare worker charged with child sex

     crimes released on reduced bond retrieved from

     https://truecrimedaily.com/2018/08/22/ex-church-daycare-wor

UPI, December 6, 2017 Time' s 2017 Person of the Year:

     ' The Silence Breakers' retrieved from

     https://newsline.com/time039s-2017-person-of-the-year

     USA TODAY, across the nation, priest sexual abuse cases

     haunt: Jerod MacDonald-Evoy, The Arizona Republic; Ken

     Stickney, the (Lafayette, La.) Daily Advertiser; Margie

     Fishman, the (Wilmington, Del.), News Journal; Stephanie

     Dickrell, St. Cloud (Minn.) Times; Jorge Fitz Gibbon,

     Poughkeepsie, Journal; Sean Lahman, Rochester (N.Y.)

     Democrat and Chronicle; Amber Sandhu, Redding (Calif.)

     Record Searchlight; Joel Shannon, York (Pa.) Daily Record;

     Courtney Crowder, The Des Moines Register; Greg Toppo,

     Retrieved from

     https://www.usatoday.com/story/news/2017/08/23/priest-sex

Acknowledgements

Walker, B. Former teacher targets three students, convicted of sex crimes retrieved from https://www.kgun9.com/news/local-new

Wagner, M., Ries, B., Yeung, J. and Levenson, E., CNN Bill Cosby sentenced to 3 to 10 years retrieved from https://www.cnn.com/us/live-news/bill-cosby-sentencing/index

WARREN, L. No one will ever be convicted of Jon Benet Ramsey's murder, says lead detective as he admits cops made a string of 'big mistakes' article retrieved from https://www.dailymail.co.uk/news/article-2969242/Detective-J

WBTW Staff, Former SC youth pastor charged with sex crimes against teen girls retrieved from https://www.wspa.com/news/former-sc-youth-pastor-charged

WILKINSON, J. Man, 51, is arrested on child sex charges after TWELVE girls are rescued from his home, including 14-year-old with whom he fathered two children after she was gifted to him by her Amish parents article retrieved from https://www.dailymail.co.uk/news/article-3647657/Three-held-Pennsylvania-rape-case-teen-Amish-girl-gifted-man.html

"Zaman, A" Congresswoman Says Two Current Lawmakers Engaged in Sexual Harassment, retrieved from http://www.carbonated.tv/news/jackie-speier-two-current-lawmakers-engaged-sexual-harassment